Death on the Nile

AGATHA CHRISTIE

Level 5

Retold by Nancy Taylor
Series Editors: Andy Hopkins and Jocelyn Potter

Contents

Introduction

'She cares too much, that little one,' Poirot said to himself. 'It is not safe. No, it is not safe.'

Early in this extremely popular mystery story, Agatha Christie's most famous detective, Hercule Poirot, observes an imbalance in the relationship between two young lovers in a London restaurant. He fears – and we, the readers, fear with him – that there is danger ahead. From the beginning of the novel, the author carefully builds a complicated plot that mixes murder and love, theft and politics. We are presented with an exciting adventure story that, like all great murder mysteries, keeps us guessing until the final pages. Look for clues as you read, but be prepared for more than a few surprises!

Born in the town of Torquay in the south of England on 15 September 1890, Dame* Agatha Christie was the leading British writer of mystery novels during her lifetime, and has remained extraordinarily popular since her death in 1976. Her books have been translated into many languages, and her play *The Mousetrap* has run continuously in London for more than fifty years. How did she become such an amazing and long-lasting success?

As a child, Agatha Christie was given the freedom to discover the world and her talent. She was educated at home, taught herself to read, and could choose her own books and form her own ideas. At the age of sixteen she went to her first formal school, in Paris, to complete her education.

Later in life Dame Agatha said that she had not planned to be

---

* Dame: a title given to a woman as a special honour for her work

a writer, but by the time she was eleven years old she had already had a poem printed in the local newspaper, and before she was twenty several more of her poems had been published in *The Poetry Review* and she had written a number of short stories.

In 1914 the First World War began and Agatha married Archibald Christie. She worked in a hospital during the war, and from this experience she gained knowledge of poisons. This proved useful when she started writing detective stories: forty-one of her novels and twenty-four short stories contain murder by poison! At about the same time as the Christies' only child, Rosalind, was born in 1919, Agatha's sister encouraged her to begin a serious writing career. She recognised Agatha's ability and dared her to write a mystery novel.

The young writer decided that she needed a detective and, as in the war-time hospital, she noticed details in the world around her. At the time her home town was full of former First World War officers and soldiers from Belgium, and Agatha decided that one of them would make the perfect model for Hercule Poirot. He starred in her first detective novel, *The Mysterious Affair at Styles* (1920).

Over the years Agatha Christie wrote about several different detectives, but Poirot had no equal in the hearts of her readers until she created Miss Marple, based partly on her own grandmother. She did not plan to put Miss Marple into a series of books, but the public loved her and she eventually appeared in twelve Christie novels and twenty short stories.

Agatha Christie wrote no fewer than sixty-six detective novels and several plays in addition to the record-breaking *The Mousetrap*, as well as six novels using the name Mary Westmacott. Her extraordinary success was the result of a simple method: Christie wrote about the world she knew, noticing every detail about real, ordinary people and places. An idea for a new novel could come into her head when she was taking a walk or shopping for a new hat; she filled dozens of notebooks with ideas, plots and characters. She was, as her grandson Mathew Prichard has described her '... a person who listened more than she talked, who saw more than she was seen.'

Agatha Christie's other great interest was the Middle East, which she learned to love when she began travelling with her second husband, Max Mallowan, in the 1930s. She loved the desert, where she and Max studied the lives of ancient peoples. She helped with these serious explorations and also used the places in some of her favourite books, especially in *Death on the Nile, Murder in Mesopotamia* and *They Came to Baghdad*. She wrote enthusiastically about her travels in this part of the world in the book that ended her long writing career: the story of her own life, which came out the year after her death.

Towards the end of their careers, both Agatha Christie and Max Mallowan were honoured by the British government for their work. Agatha became a Dame in 1971. This honour came from a nation that was grateful for her entertaining stories, and also for the fact that she helped to define the English character and way of life for the rest of the world.

Death on the Nile brings together many of the best features of an Agatha Christie novel: murder, a colourful foreign background, a group of interesting suspects, and a surprising solution by the amazing Monsieur Hercule Poirot. It is not surprising that Dame Agatha's detective novels continue to charm and entertain millions of readers around the world. The popularity of her stories goes beyond the printed page. There have been many television and film productions of her mysteries, and there is even a very popular computer game based on *Death on the Nile*. Doubtless Agatha Christie's stories will continue to excite readers and audiences for many, many years.

Hercule Poirot, the famous Belgian detective.

Chapter 1 Egypt! An Excellent Destination!

'Look! That's *her*! Linnet Ridgeway! She's got millions,' said Mr Burnaby, the owner of the local pub.

He and his only customer stared as a beautiful young woman jumped out of a large Rolls Royce and hurried into the post office. Such charming girls were seldom seen in the sleepy town of Malton-under-Wode.

'She'll bring money into the town,' remarked the man at the bar. 'A bit different from Sir George.'

'That's true. He had no luck, especially with the horses.'

'What did she pay for his house?'

'About sixty thousand, and she's going to spend that much on changes to the place.'

'No! Where did she get all that money from?'

'From an American grandfather, Leopold Hartz,' Mr Burnaby informed him. 'He left millions to his daughter, who married Melhuish Ridgeway. Like a Hollywood film, isn't it?'

They watched the girl leave the post office and drive off.

'Money *and* good looks,' complained the man at the bar. 'It doesn't seem fair ... '

◆

'Darling, I think this place is going to be quite *wonderful*!'

The Hon.* Joanna Southwood was sitting in Linnet Ridgeway's bedroom at Wode Hall.

'It's perfect, isn't it? agreed Linnet.

Her face was enthusiastic and alive. Joanna's long, clever face and strange eye make-up couldn't compete with Linnet's

---

* Hon.: the Honourable, a title that the children of some English lords and ladies are allowed to use

natural beauty.

Joanna picked up a beautiful string of pearls. 'I suppose these are real, aren't they, Linnet?'

'Of course.'

'Most people can't afford real pearls, my dear. These are *amazing*. What *are* they worth?'

'About fifty thousand.'

'Aren't you afraid of having them stolen?'

'No, I always wear them, and anyway they're insured.'

'Let me wear them until dinner time, will you, darling? It would be so exciting!'

Linnet laughed 'Of course, if you'd like to.'

Joanna put on the pearls and said, 'I really envy you, Linnet. You've got *everything*: money, beauty, perfect health. You've even got *brains*! When's your twenty-first birthday?'

'Next June. I'll have a big, brilliant party in London.'

'And then are you going to marry Charles Windlesham? The newspapers are so excited about the possibility. His big old house could use your attention. Just think! You could rule both Wode Hall and Charltonbury. And he *is* in love with you.'

'I don't really want to marry anyone yet,' Linnet replied.

A telephone call from Jacqueline de Bellefort, Linnet's oldest friend, interrupted their pleasant conversation.

'Jackie!' Linnet shouted. 'I haven't heard from you for *ages*!'

'Darling, I apologize, but now I want to see you urgently,' her friend said. 'Can I come down?'

'Yes, please! I'd love to show you Wode Hall.'

'Right. If my old car isn't in a bad mood, I'll see you in time for afternoon tea. Goodbye, darling!'

'Jackie and I were at school together in Paris,' Linnet told Joanna. 'Her father ran off and left the family without a penny.'

'Darling,' Joanna said, 'if *my* friends lose their money, I stop seeing them *immediately*! They always want to borrow from me.'

'So if *I* lost all my money tomorrow?' asked Linnet.

'Darling, you'd never see me again. Nobody wants poor, unsuccessful friends.'

'Joanna, you're terrible! And you're wrong about Jacqueline. She's very proud and has never asked me for money.'

'Let's wait and see. I suspect she wants something,' Joanna warned her.

'She *did* sound excited,' admitted Linnet. 'She always does.'

At that moment, one of Linnet's servants entered the room. She apologized quietly and left with a dress from Linnet's cupboard.

'Has Marie been crying?' asked Joanna.

'Poor Marie! She was planning to marry a man who has a job in Egypt. She didn't know much about him, so I made some enquiries. He has a wife already – and three children.'

'You must make a lot of enemies, Linnet. You're so wonderfully efficient and so good at doing the right thing.'

Linnet laughed. 'I haven't got an enemy in the world!'

♦

At four o'clock Jacqueline de Bellefort found her friend, Linnet, and Lord Windlesham in the grand sitting-room at Wode Hall. The gentleman watched the girls greet each other affectionately. A pretty child, he thought – not beautiful, but definitely attractive, with her dark curly hair and her enormous eyes. He politely greeted the girl and then left the two friends alone.

Jacqueline asked excitedly, '*Lord* Windlesham? The man the newspapers always say you're going to marry? *Are* you?'

'I'm not ready to decide. Now, let's talk about *you*. Where have you been? Why haven't you written?'

'I've been at work. You see, I have to have a job.'

'But darling, why didn't you …? ' Linnet began.

'Ask you for help? Well, that's what I'm here for. Not to

borrow money, but I have a great big important request.'

'Go on,' encouraged Linnet. 'Tell me about it.'

'If you're going to marry Windlesham, perhaps you'll understand. I'm engaged to a man called Simon Doyle. He's simple and boyish and charming and completely loveable! He's got no money – but he's from a good family. He's been in a terribly boring office job, and now he's lost that. Linnet, I shall *die* if I can't marry him!

'Don't be silly, Jackie!'

'No, I'm not exaggerating. We can't live without each other. Listen, I want you to give the job of land agent at Wode Hall to Simon. It's perfect for him. And if he's no good, you can sack him. My special Linnet, my dear friend, say you'll hire him!'

Linnet laughed. 'Jackie, you really *are* mad! Bring this young man to Wode Hall and we'll talk about it.'

'*Darling* Linnet! I'll bring him tomorrow. You'll love him!'

♦

In London that evening, as Jacqueline de Bellefort and her young man, Simon Doyle, celebrated at Chez Ma Tante, the owner of that restaurant welcomed an important guest. To most observers, this small, strange-looking man with a big moustache looked nothing like an important customer, but Monsieur* Blondin quickly found a very good table for his special friend.

'Monsieur Poirot!' Monsieur Blondin greeted the new arrival. 'It is wonderful to see you.'

Hercule Poirot, the famous Belgian detective, smiled, remembering a case in which a dead body, a waiter, Monsieur Blondin and a very attractive lady had all played a part.

Monsieur Blondin lowered his voice. 'Are you working on

---

* Monsieur: French for *Mr* or *sir*; Madame is the word for *Mrs* or *madam*, and Mademoiselle (plural: Mesdemoiselles) is the word for *Miss*.

something serious now?'

Poirot shook his head. 'I have, unfortunately, retired. It is true, however, that man invented work to avoid having to think, but there is travel. This winter I shall visit Egypt – the climate, they say, is good.'

'Egypt! An excellent destination!'

Monsieur Poirot watched the dancers, and smiled when he noticed one particular couple: a tall, handsome man with broad shoulders and a thin, dark-haired girl. Their happiness – in the place, the time and in each other – was obvious.

The music stopped and the couple returned to a table near Monsieur Poirot. The girl was bright-eyed, laughing, but there was something else in her eyes.

'She cares too much, that little one,' Poirot said to himself. 'It is not safe. No, it is not safe.' And then a word caught his attention: 'Egypt.' He listened more carefully.

'Don't worry, Simon,' the girl said. 'Linnet won't disappoint us.'

'The job sounds perfect. And I will work hard – for *you*!'

'We'll wait for three months,' the girl said happily.

'Then, everything that is mine will be yours,' the young man said. 'And Egypt for our honeymoon! Never mind the cost. I've always wanted to go there. The Nile and the Pyramids ... We'll see it together, Jackie. Won't it be wonderful?'

'Yes,' the girl replied, and her voice was suddenly sharp, almost with fear. 'But will it be as wonderful for you as for me?'

'Don't be silly, Jackie. Let's dance.'

'*Une qui aime et un qui se laisse aimer,*'* Monsieur Poirot thought. 'Yes, I wonder too.'

◆

* *une qui aime et un qui se laisse aimer*: French for 'a woman who loves, and a man who allows himself to be loved'

'What will you do if he's awful?' asked Joanna.

Linnet shook her head. 'Oh, I can trust Jacqueline's taste.'

'Ah, but love changes people,' Joanna said quietly.

Linnet looked impatient and changed the subject. 'I must talk to the architect about those plans. I'm having some horrible little houses near my new swimming pool pulled down.'

'Are the people who live in them happy to go?'

'Most of them are delighted. One or two of them are being rather stupid about it. They'll have much better living conditions.'

'The queen has spoken,' smiled Joanna.

'I'm not like that!' objected Linnet.

'No, but others are powerless. The combined effect of money and charm. If you can't buy it with cash, you buy it with a smile. Result: Linnet Ridgeway, The Girl Who Has Everything.'

Their conversation stopped as Lord Windlesham joined them. Joanna greeted him and then left the sitting-room. She had seen the purposeful look in Windlesham's eye.

'Have you made a decision, Linnet?' he asked, coming straight to the point. 'I think, you know, we'd be very happy together.'

'I'm not sure, Charles,' Linnet apologized. 'I'm enjoying myself. I do think Wode Hall is looking nice, don't you?'

'It's beautiful. And you like Charltonbury, don't you? Of course it needs modernizing – but you're so clever at that sort of thing.' He paused. 'But I'll wait for your answer.'

Later, Linnet examined her feelings. Charltonbury was beautiful, old and quite famous, but it wasn't *hers*. There, she would be Lord Windlesham's wife, not the queen.

And wasn't there another reason for her hesitation? She remembered Jackie's voice, saying, 'I shall *die* if I can't marry him!' She knew that she didn't feel that way about Charles Windlesham. Perhaps she could never feel like that about anyone.

The sound of a car came through the open window. Linnet

shook herself impatiently and went to greet Jackie and her young man.

'Linnet!' Jackie ran to her. 'This is Simon!'

Linnet saw a tall, wide-shouldered young man with very dark blue eyes, curly brown hair and a simple, boyish smile ... She stretched out her hand. The hand that took hers was firm and warm. She liked the open admiration in his eyes, and a warm, sweet feeling swept over her.

'Come in!' she said, as she finally dropped Simon's hand. 'Let me welcome my new land agent properly.'

And as she turned to lead the way, she thought, 'I'm very, very happy. I like Jackie's young man ... I like him enormously ...'

And then, sadly: 'Lucky Jackie ... '

◆

On the Spanish island of Majorca, Tim Allerton leant back in his chair and yawned. He looked at the attractive, white-haired woman of fifty who sat beside him.

'Do you really like Majorca, Mother?' he asked.

'Well,' his mother said after some consideration, 'it's cheap.'

'And cold.'

Tim was a tall, thin young man with dark hair and sad eyes. He described himself as a writer, but his friends understood that he did not encourage questions about his work.

'What are you thinking of, Tim?'

'I was thinking of Egypt. Real warmth, darling. Golden sands. The Nile. You mustn't worry about the cost. I heard this morning that I've made a very satisfactory amount from an investment.'

'This morning?' said Mrs Allerton. 'But your only letter this morning was from Joanna ...' She stopped and bit her lip.

The friendship between her son and his cousin always annoyed her. They both liked discussing others, and had many of the same friends. Mrs Allerton didn't like to admit that she felt slightly jealous of the girl. 'But it's more than that,' she thought. 'I don't like her. She's insincere, and can't be serious about anything.'

'Quite right, Mother,' he said coolly. 'It was yesterday that I heard about the investment. Here's Joanna's letter – it's full of news. Windlesham's gone to Canada, upset by Linnet Ridgeway's refusal. She's definitely going to marry her land agent. He has no money, of course, though he's from a good family, and he was actually engaged to one of Linnet's best friends.'

'Young people today don't know how to behave,' said Mrs Allerton. 'And is Joanna enjoying life?'

'She says she's thinking of opening a little shop in Mayfair.'

'She always talks about having no money, but she travels and her clothes must cost her a lot.'

'Ah,' said Tim, 'but she probably doesn't pay for them.'

'Well, unpaid bills lead to ruin in the end. Think about poor Sir George Wode. He's suffered terribly since he lost Wode Hall. He thinks Linnet Ridgeway has spoilt the place, and robbed his family of their history.'

'But Mother, he shouldn't live in the past and neither should we! We'll go to Egypt next month. No arguments!'

Mrs Allerton smiled affectionately, and then said guiltily, 'I'm afraid I promised Mrs Leech that you'd go with her to the police station. She wants to report the robbery of her ring, but she doesn't understand any Spanish.'

'I'll go, but the silly old woman was wearing the ring when she went swimming that day. I'm sure she lost it in the sea.'

◆

In a New York apartment, old Miss Van Schuyler addressed her poor relations.

'I'm going to Europe and then to Egypt,' the old woman

explained. 'Miss Bowers will come with me as usual, but I want Cornelia to come as my social assistant.'

'How wonderful!' cried Cornelia Robson, a large girl with big doglike eyes. 'I've always dreamed of a trip to Europe.'

'My dear cousin,' her mother added, rising to leave, 'I'm really *very* grateful to you. I think Cornelia suffers from not being a social success here in New York. I haven't been able to take her to the right places since Ned died.'

As the Robsons were leaving, they met a tall, efficient-looking woman on the stairs.

'Well, Miss Bowers, so you're going to Egypt? What a lovely trip!' Mrs Robson hesitated, and waited until her daughter had gone on ahead of her. 'I do hope there won't be any ... trouble,' she whispered with concern.

'Oh, *no*, Mrs Robson. I always watch *very* carefully.'

♦

In another part of New York City, Mr Andrew Pennington was opening his personal mail. Suddenly, his face changed and he called for his partner.

'What is it, Pennington?' Sterndale Rockford looked not unlike his partner – tall and thin with greying hair and a clever face.

'Linnet's married.' Pennington checked the date. 'Today. To someone called Simon Doyle. I've never heard of him, have you?'

'No. What shall we do?' Rockford asked. 'Got a plan?'

'The *Normandie* sails for Europe today,' Pennington said slowly. He looked at the letter again. 'Linnet's going to Egypt for her honeymoon. A chance meeting there? We have to stay one step ahead of her British lawyers.'

'Linnet's clever,' said Rockford. '*You* go. She's always liked you – her "Uncle Andrew". And the situation is very serious.'

♦

In the London offices of Carmichael, Grant and Carmichael, William Carmichael called his nephew into *his* office.

'Have a quick look at this letter,' he said to young Jim Fanthorp. 'It's just arrived by airmail from Egypt.'

... It seems wrong to be writing business letters on a day like this. We have been to so many interesting places already and the day after tomorrow we are going up the Nile by steamboat. When we went to buy our tickets, who do you think we saw? My American trustee, Andrew Pennington. I think you met him when he was in London two years ago. I had no idea he was in Egypt and he had no idea that I was! Nor that I was married! My letter, telling him, must have just missed him. He is actually going up the Nile on the same trip that we are. Isn't that amazing? ...

'You must go to Egypt.' Carmichael interrupted his nephew's reading. 'There's no time to lose.'

'But why me?'

'Use your brains, boy. Linnet Ridgeway has never met you; nor has Pennington. If you go by air, you may get there in time.'

♦

Mrs Otterbourne addressed her daughter in her usual theatrical manner as she tied a brightly coloured scarf around her head.

'I'm tired of Jerusalem,' she complained. 'And I'm not treated with the proper respect in this hotel. My presence here attracts other visitors! Rosalie, are you listening to me?'

Rosalie was silent – she was looking at a photograph in the newspaper, below which was printed:

Mrs Simon Doyle, previously the well-known society beauty Miss Linnet Ridgeway, and her husband. Mr and Mrs Doyle are on their honeymoon in Egypt.

'That nasty little manager,' Mrs Otterbourne continued, 'says he needs our room, but I'm prepared to fight for my rights.'

'I suppose we could go on to Egypt,' said Rosalie, without much interest. 'It doesn't make any difference.'

'It's certainly not a matter of life or death,' agreed her mother.

But Mrs Otterbourne was quite wrong – because a matter of life or death was exactly what it was.

Chapter 2   Who's Who on the Nile

'That's Hercule Poirot, the detective,' said Mrs Allerton.

She and her son were sitting in the sun outside the Cataract Hotel in Assuan. Tim sat up more quickly than he usually did.

'That funny little man in the white suit? What's *he* doing here?'

His mother laughed. 'Darling, you sound quite excited. But I don't think he's looking for criminals. He's probably on holiday.'

'Well, he's found the best-looking girl in the place,' Tim noted. 'It's a pity that she looks so bad-tempered.'

The subject of these remarks was Rosalie Otterbourne. She certainly seemed to be in a bad mood, but Hercule Poirot was chatting to her cheerfully.

'I am finding this place very interesting,' he was saying. 'The black rocks, and the sun, and the little boats on the river.'

'I think Assuan's rather dull,' Rosalie said. 'The hotel's half empty and everyone's about a hundred years old.' She stopped as she saw the smile in Poirot's eyes. 'I – I wasn't thinking of you. I'm sorry. That sounded rude.'

'Please, do not apologize,' said Poirot. 'It is natural that you should wish for people of your own age. But there is *one* young man, at least.'

'The one who sits with his mother all the time? I like *her*, but I think he looks awful – so arrogant.'

'And I – am *I* arrogant?'

'Oh, I don't think so, and anyway, I suppose you have a reason to be arrogant. Unfortunately, crime doesn't interest me at all.'

Poirot said seriously, 'I am delighted to learn that you have no guilty secret to hide.' Rosalie looked questioningly at Poirot, but the detective did not seem to notice, and continued, 'We will both make the trip to Wadi* Halfa and the Second Cataract?† And Madame, your mother, was not at lunch today. I hope that she is able to join us.'

'Egypt doesn't suit her,' Rosalie said quickly, 'but we will be on the trip.'

They continued their walk to the river's edge. One of the Nile steamboats was just arriving, and Poirot and Rosalie looked at the passengers with interest. Tim Allerton joined them.

'Look!' he shouted excitedly. 'That's Linnet Ridgeway. There with the tall man. He must be the new husband.'

'Doyle,' said Rosalie. 'Simon Doyle. It was in the newspapers. She's got an enormous amount of money, hasn't she?'

'Yes,' Tim agreed. 'She's probably the richest girl in England.'

Linnet Ridgeway, now Linnet Doyle, stepped off the boat with the confidence of a famous actress who expects people to admire her. Then she made a light remark to her husband, and when he answered, the sound of his voice seemed to interest Hercule Poirot. His eyes lit up.

The couple passed close to him and he heard Simon Doyle say, 'We can stay a week or two if you like, darling.' He was looking at her with a deeply loving, almost respectful attitude.

---

* wadi: a dry valley or riverbed
† cataract: a large or high waterfall

Poirot's eyes considered him thoughtfully.

Tim watched the couple too. 'Lucky devil! Most girls with millions have something wrong with them. She's perfect!'

'They look truly happy,' commented Rosalie. 'It isn't fair,' she added quietly.

She and Poirot continued their walk. 'So, it is not fair, Mademoiselle?' asked the detective gently.

Rosalie's face turned red. 'It seems a little too much for one person,' she said. 'Money, good looks, a beautiful figure and –'

'And love? But perhaps he married her for her money.'

'Didn't you see the way he looked at her?'

'I also saw dark circles below her eyes. I saw a hand that held her bag so tightly that it was white. Something is not right. And I know something else,' the detective continued. 'I have heard the voice of Monsieur Doyle before.'

But Rosalie was not listening. 'I'd like to tear her beautiful clothes off her back and destroy her lovely, arrogant face. I'm just jealous – I've never hated anyone so much at first sight.'

'Wonderful! You will feel better after saying all that.'

Rosalie looked at him doubtfully. Then they both laughed, and made their way slowly back to the hotel.

Poirot found a seat in the garden, and was looking around him when he recognized the girl from Chez Ma Tante. The expression on her face now was very different. She was paler, thinner, and there were lines that told of great unhappiness. A face – and a voice. The new husband, Mr Simon Doyle, had been at Chez Ma Tante with this young woman.

Suddenly, Linnet Doyle and her husband came down the path. Linnet's voice was happy and confident. The girl from Chez Ma Tante stepped into the path.

The other two stopped.

'Hello, Linnet,' said Jacqueline de Bellefort. 'Our paths keep crossing. Hello, Simon, how are you?'

Linnet had moved back with a little cry. Anger completely changed Simon Doyle's good-looking face. He looked ready to hit the girl, but then he noticed Poirot.

'Hello, Jacqueline,' he said coldly. 'What a surprise.'

'A surprise?' she asked. Then she walked away.

Poirot left in the opposite direction. He heard Linnet Doyle say, 'Simon! What can we do? Oh, what can we do?'

♦

After dinner that night, most of the guests at the Cataract Hotel were sitting at little tables on the terrace. Simon and Linnet Doyle and a tall, serious-looking, grey-haired American hesitated in the doorway. Tim Allerton rose from his chair and greeted them.

'You don't remember me, I'm sure,' he said pleasantly to Linnet, 'but I'm Joanna Southwood's cousin.'

'Of course I remember you! You're Tim Allerton. This is my husband.' Her voice shook slightly – pride, shyness? 'And this is my American trustee, Mr Andrew Pennington.'

The three new arrivals joined Tim and his mother at a table. The next time the doors opened, Linnet looked up nervously, but relaxed as a small man came out and walked across the terrace.

'You're not the only celebrity here, my dear. That funny little man is Hercule Poirot,' explained Mrs Allerton.

'Of course,' said Linnet thoughtfully. 'I've heard of him … '

'Monsieur Poirot!' called Mrs Otterbourne, in her loud, bossy voice, from the other side of the terrace. 'Sit down with us.' He obeyed. 'There are quite a lot of celebrities here now, aren't there? Society beauties, well-known detectives, famous novelists.'

Poirot felt rather than saw Rosalie's unhappiness. 'You are working on a novel at present, Madame?' he asked politely.

'I'm being terribly lazy,' Mrs Otterbourne said. 'My readers are getting very impatient. I'll soon start writing again. I speak the truth. Sex – ah! Monsieur Poirot, why is everyone so afraid of sex? You have read my books?'

'Ah, Madame, I do not read many novels. My work ...'

Mrs Otterbourne interrupted. 'You must have a copy of *Under the Fig Tree*. You will find it interesting. It's honest – and *real*.'

'I'll fetch the book for you,' offered Rosalie quickly.

'No, dear, I can go,' said Mrs Otterbourne angrily.

'Please, Mother, talk to Monsieur Poirot. I know where it is.'

'A glass of wine, Madame?' offered Poirot, when Rosalie had left.

'No, no, I rarely touch alcohol.'

'Then may I order a lemonade for you, Madame?'

Rosalie returned, a book in her hand. Poirot was surprised by the lack of clothes worn by the lady on the cover, but he accepted it politely while noticing the girl's embarrassment.

Suddenly, the doors opened again and the thin, dark-haired girl from Chez Ma Tante walked quietly to an empty table and chose her seat carefully. Then she stared directly at Linnet Doyle. Linnet whispered something to Mr Pennington and changed her seat.

Poirot noticed everything and wondered about the situation.

Five minutes later, the other girl moved to the opposite side of the terrace. Her eyes never left the face of Simon Doyle's wife.

Soon Linnet Doyle and her husband left the terrace. Jacqueline de Bellefort smiled and lit a cigarette.

♦

'Monsieur Poirot?'

Poirot stood up quickly. He had remained out on the terrace after everyone else had left. He looked into the eyes of Linnet

Doyle, who looked more lovely than ever.

'At your service, Madame,' he said politely.

'Monsieur Poirot, I am in urgent need of someone to help me. And I think that you are probably the right person.'

'Thank you, Madame, but I am on holiday, and when I am on holiday I do not take cases.'

'Perhaps I can change that,' Linnet said confidently. 'Before I met my husband, he was engaged to a close friend of mine, Miss de Bellefort. My husband ended the engagement – they were not suited to each other. Miss de Bellefort, I am sorry to say, was very unhappy about it. She threatened us, but didn't harm us. Instead, she has begun to follow us wherever we go.'

'Ah – rather an unusual – er – revenge,' commented Poirot.

'Unusual – and annoying. We're on our honeymoon and she has been there at every stop: Venice, Brindisi, Mena House and now here. It's nonsensical. I am surprised she hasn't got more pride.'

'There are times, Madame, when other emotions are stronger.'

'Yes, possibly, but what can she hope to *gain* by all this?'

'It is not always a matter of gain, Madame.'

Linnet looked slightly embarrassed but said quickly, 'You are right, but this behaviour has got to be stopped.'

'If this young lady has not threatened or insulted you in public and if she has not physically harmed you, I do not see what you can do. The air is free to all!'

'This is impossible! There *must* be some way of stopping her.'

'You could move somewhere else,' said Poirot calmly.

'Why should we – run away? Are we … ?' She stopped.

'Exactly, Madame. Are you … what? Why does Mademoiselle de Bellefort's presence offend you so much? I will tell you a little story. A month or two ago, I was dining in a restaurant in London. At the table next to me were a man and a girl. They

16

were, it seemed, very much in love and confident of the future. I could see the woman's face, and the strength of her love was clear. They were engaged, I learnt, and were discussing their honeymoon. They planned to go to Egypt.' He paused. 'And now they are here, in Egypt. But the man is on his honeymoon with another woman.'

'Yes, I had already told you the facts,' said Linnet coldly.

Poirot continued, 'The facts – yes. But that night in London, the girl also mentioned a friend who she could depend on. I think that friend was you, Madame. She trusted you.'

'These things happen, Monsieur Poirot,' Linnet said angrily. 'I know that Jackie was deeply in love with Simon, but he didn't feel the same way. He was very fond of her, but even before he met me, he was beginning to feel that he had made a mistake – and an engagement can be broken.'

'Your argument is logical,' said Poirot, 'but it does not explain one thing – your attitude. Your very close friend has been deeply hurt, but instead of feeling pity or annoyance at her behaviour, you are extremely angry. There can be only one reason for your reaction – that you feel a sense of guilt.'

Linnet jumped to her feet. 'How dare you talk to me like that! Really, Monsieur Poirot!'

'But I *do* dare, Madame. I suggest that you felt strongly attracted to Simon Doyle at once. Then there was a moment when you had a *choice*. You hesitated, but you chose to use your charm to take Simon from your friend, although you knew what he meant to her.'

There was a silence. Then Linnet said in a cold voice, 'This has nothing to do with my problem now.'

'I disagree with you, Madame. I am explaining why your friend's unexpected appearances upset you so much. You know, in your heart, that she has right on her side. I am guessing that you have had a happy life, that you have been kind and generous in your attitude to others.'

'I have tried to be,' said Linnet quietly.

'And that is why you are so upset that you have intentionally caused someone pain. I am sorry if I have been rude, but psychology is the most important fact in a case.'

Linnet said slowly, 'Perhaps you're right – but what can be done about it *now*? I can't change the past.'

'You must accept that you are responsible for your friend's problems. You must have courage and do nothing.'

'Couldn't you – talk to Jackie? Try to reason with her?'

'What is your husband's attitude to this situation?'

'He's angry,' said Linnet. 'Extremely angry.'

Poirot considered this. 'Well, I will talk to this young woman as a private individual, but I do not believe that I shall achieve anything. Tell me, how did she threaten you?'

'She threatened to kill us both.'

♦

Hercule Poirot found Jacqueline de Bellefort sitting on the rocks below the terrace.

'Mademoiselle,' he began, 'may I talk to you? I have just come from Madame Doyle – but I am not working for her.'

'Oh! Then why have you come?'

'I saw you and Monsieur Doyle once at Chez Ma Tante,' Poirot explained. 'Since then, many things have happened. You cannot change the past. Turn to the future and stop this suffering.'

'I am sure that would suit dear Linnet,' Jacqueline said angrily. 'But there are times when I almost enjoy all of this.'

'And that, Mademoiselle, is the worst of all,' Poirot said gently. 'Go home. You have your whole life in front of you.'

'Monsieur Poirot, I love Simon – and he loves me … And I loved Linnet … and trusted her. She was my best friend. But she has always been able to buy everything she wanted.'

'Did Monsieur Doyle allow himself to be bought?'

'No, it's more complicated than that. She gave up Lord Windlesham and his title and his big house and chose Simon. He felt confused, but also special. Linnet's beauty and charm blinded him, and he couldn't see me any more. He fell in love with her because she made him.' She looked away. 'Yes, he hates me now. But he'd better be careful.' She pulled a small pearl-handled pistol from her handbag. 'A nice little thing. One bullet would kill a man or a woman, and I know how to use it. I was going to shoot them, but then I decided to follow them and steal their happiness.' She laughed loudly.

Poirot took her arm. 'Stop this!' he said. 'Do not open your heart to evil. It will make its home there and destroy you.'

Jacqueline hesitated, but then said, 'You couldn't stop me if I decided to kill her. What have I got to live for?'

'But, Mademoiselle, murder is an unforgivable offence.'

'Then you should respect my present method of revenge. As long as it works, I won't use that gun. But sometimes I want to hurt her – to put my little pistol against her head and shoot her – Oh!' She stared into the shadows. 'Someone was standing there.'

Poirot looked round quickly. The place seemed completely empty. 'I think we are alone, Mademoiselle.'

'You do understand – that I can't do what you ask.'

Poirot shook his head. 'But you can! There is always a moment. You could be different from your friend Linnet, and make the right choice. If that moment passes, there is no second chance.'

'No second chance ...' Jacqueline looked thoughtful, then raised her head. 'Good night, Monsieur Poirot.'

♦

The next morning, Simon Doyle joined Hercule Poirot as the detective was walking into the town.

'Good morning, Monsieur Poirot. May I walk with you?'

'Certainly, Monsieur Doyle. I shall be delighted.'

Simon hesitated and then said suddenly, 'This problem that Linnet told you about – it's a crime that she should be treated this way! People can say that I behaved badly, but I won't allow them to blame her.'

'Did you – have you talked to Jackie – Miss de Bellefort?'

'Yes, but she wouldn't listen. Can't she see that she's making a fool of herself?' demanded Simon.

'She has only a sense of – injury, shall we say?' Poirot replied.

'Yes, and I would understand if she never wished to see me again. I admit I was completely to blame. But respectable girls don't follow people round. What can she hope to gain from it?'

'Perhaps – revenge!'

'Crazy! I'd understand better if she tried to shoot me,' said Simon. 'She's hot-blooded – and she's got an uncontrollable temper. She could do anything for revenge if she were really angry. But this spying ...'

'It is cleverer – yes! It is intelligent! And there is nothing, then, of the old feeling left?' asked Poirot carefully.

'Monsieur Poirot, how can I explain it? After I met Linnet, Jackie didn't exist. She thinks that I married Linnet for her money, but I wouldn't marry any woman for money! I know this sounds arrogant, but Jackie was *too* fond of me!'

'*Une qui aime et un qui se laisse aimer,*' remarked Poirot.

Simon ignored this comment. 'Jackie wanted to own me, body and soul, and a man doesn't want that kind of possessive attitude. Then I met Linnet.' His voice was full of boyish wonder. 'It was amazing. Everyone treats her like a queen – and she chose me. I'm nobody! Why can't Jackie accept it like a man?'

Poirot's upper lip curled in a faint smile. 'Well, Monsieur Doyle, she is *not* a man.'

'No, but she should understand the situation. If you no longer care for a girl, it's madness to marry her. And now that I can see what Jackie's really like, I feel I've had rather a lucky escape.'

'Have you any idea what else she would do?' Poirot asked thoughtfully. 'She carries a pistol in her handbag.'

Simon looked surprised. 'I don't believe she'll use it – she threatened earlier, but the situation has gone past that. This spying on us and following us everywhere has really hurt Linnet. But I've made a plan. I've announced openly that we're going to stay here for ten days. But tomorrow the steamboat *Karnak* starts from Shellal to Wadi Halfa. I'll book our tickets for that trip under false names. Tomorrow morning Linnet and I will leave the hotel, saying that we're going to Philae for the day, but instead we'll go to Shellal and join the *Karnak* there. Linnet's maid will bring our luggage. Jackie will expect us back at the hotel in the evening, but when we don't return, it will be too late for her to find us.'

'And if Miss de Bellefort waits here until you return?'

'We may not return. We could go to Khartoum and then perhaps by air to Kenya. She can't follow us all round the world.'

'Your plan may work,' said Poirot, 'but you are, of course, running away from the problem. And remember, Mademoiselle de Bellefort has brains.' Then he added, 'I, too, shall be on the *Karnak*. I bought my ticket in London. I like to plan every detail.'

Simon laughed. 'Is that how a skilful murderer behaves? You must tell us about some of your cases when we're on the *Karnak*. I know that Mrs Allerton would like to hear about your work.'

'Mrs Allerton? That is the charming white-haired woman who has such a loving son?'

'Yes. She'll be on the *Karnak* too, but she doesn't know about my plan. I believe that it's better not to trust anybody.'

'Very wise. A principle I also follow. And the third member of your party, the tall grey-haired man …'

'That's Pennington, Linnet's American trustee. We met him by chance in Cairo.'

'*Ah, vraiment!** A question, with your permission? Madame – your wife – is over twenty-one years old?'

'No, not yet, but she didn't need anyone's permission to marry me. It was a great surprise to Pennington. He left New York on the *Carmanic* two days before her letter about our wedding reached his office.'

'The *Carmanic* ... ' Poirot said thoughtfully. 'What a coincidence to meet Mr Pennington in Cairo.'

'Yes, and his plans included this Nile trip, so we've been travelling together. On our honeymoon! But at least, in his presence, we have to talk about other things, and not Jackie.'

'Your wife has not told Mr Pennington about this problem?'

'No, it's *our* problem, and anyway, when we started on this Nile trip we thought we'd seen the end of it.'

'No,' said Poirot. 'I am sure you have not yet seen the end of it.'

'You're not very encouraging, are you, Monsieur Poirot?'

Simon Doyle's attitude worried Poirot. 'This man is like a child,' he thought. 'He takes nothing seriously except playing games! But his wife and Jacqueline de Bellefort take this business seriously.'

The detective said, 'You will allow me to ask a personal question? Was it your idea to come to Egypt for your honeymoon?'

Simon seemed upset again. 'No, but Linnet absolutely insisted on it. And so – and so –'. he stopped.

'Naturally,' said Poirot. He understood that if Linnet Doyle decided on anything, it had to happen. He thought to himself, 'I have heard from Jacqueline de Bellefort, Linnet Doyle and her husband. Whose story of this affair is nearest the truth?'

---

* *Ah, vraiment!*: French for 'Oh, really!'

♦

At eleven the next morning, Jacqueline de Bellefort sat on the terrace and watched Simon and Linnet Doyle depart in a small sailboat. At the same time, and without Jacqueline seeing it, a car departed with the Doyles' luggage and Linnet's maid.

Hercule Poirot decided to spend the time before lunch on the island of Elephantine, opposite the hotel, and joined two men stepping into one of the hotel boats. The younger man was a tall, dark-haired young man with a thin, angry face. His clothes were extremely dirty and unsuitable for the climate. The other traveller, a heavy middle-aged man with a foreign accent, began a conversation with Poirot as the boat headed for Elephantine. The younger man turned his back on them, and instead admired the skill of the Egyptian boatman who was piloting the boat.

On the little island, the friendly stranger introduced himself to Monsieur Poirot as Signor* Guido Richetti, a historian. Poirot accepted his card politely and formally presented Signor Richetti with one of his own cards. Then the two men, now speaking in French, stepped into the Elephantine Museum together. The younger man from the boat walked around with little interest.

Afterwards, Poirot noticed Mrs Allerton sitting alone beside the river, and joined her. He removed his hat politely.

'Good morning, Mr Poirot,' Mrs Allerton said. 'Are you joining us on the trip to the Second Cataract?'

'Yes, I am.'

'I'm so glad. I'm very excited to meet you. But I saw you talking to Simon Doyle earlier. What do you think of him? His marriage to Linnet Ridgeway was a great surprise.'

'You know Madame Doyle well, Madame?'

'No, but a cousin of mine, Joanna Southwood, is one of her

* Signor: Italian for *Mr* or *sir*

best friends – and one of Tim's.' She looked displeased.

'You do not like your cousin, Madame?'

'Not much,' said Mrs Allerton, and then changed the subject. 'How very few young people there are out here! That pretty girl with the awful mother is almost the only young creature in the place. She interests me, that child, but I feel sorry for her. You can suffer so much when you're young and sensitive.'

'Yes,' agreed Poirot. 'She is not happy, poor little one.'

'I've tried to talk to her, but she's not interested. However, I hope to have another opportunity on this Nile trip. I'm very friendly, really – people interest me *enormously*.' She paused, then said: 'Tim tells me that the dark-haired girl, Miss de Bellefort, is the girl who was engaged to Simon Doyle. It's rather uncomfortable for them – meeting like this. You know, it may sound foolish, but she almost frightens me.'

'A great force of emotion is always frightening,' Poirot said.

'Do people interest you too, Monsieur Poirot? Or are you only interested in possible criminals?'

'That description would not leave many people outside it.'

'Even me, perhaps?' asked Mrs Allerton with surprise.

'Mothers, Madame, are particularly dangerous when their children are in trouble.'

She said seriously, 'Yes, I think you're quite right.' Then she smiled again and said, 'I'm trying to imagine motives for crime suitable for everyone in the hotel. Simon Doyle, for example?'

Poirot said, smiling, 'A very simple crime – nothing complicated. He would go directly towards his goal.'

'And therefore he would be easy to catch?'

'Yes, he would not be clever.'

'And Linnet?'

'She would act like a queen and simply give her orders.'

'And the dangerous girl – Jacqueline de Bellefort – could *she* commit a murder?'

Poirot paused and then said doubtfully, 'Yes, I think she could. I'm not sure. She puzzles me, that little one.'

'Mr Pennington couldn't commit a murder. There's no red blood in him,' said Mrs Allerton, enjoying the game. 'And poor Mrs Otterbourne in her funny clothes?'

'There is always pride.'

'As a motive for murder?' asked Mrs Allerton doubtfully.

'Motives for murder are not always grand, Madame.'

'What are the most usual motives, Monsieur Poirot?'

'Most frequent – money. Then there is revenge – and love, and fear, and pure hate, and even generosity.'

'Monsieur Poirot!'

'Oh, yes, Madame. Political murders are often in this group. Somebody is considered harmful to a society and is removed. The murderers forget that life and death are the affair of God.'

Soon they joined the others in the boat to return to the hotel. Poirot spoke politely to the young man in the dirty clothes.

'There are very wonderful things to see in Egypt, are there not?'

'They make me sick,' the young man replied in a surprisingly educated voice. 'Think of the poor workers who struggled to build all these *important* buildings, and died doing it.'

'You'd prefer to have no Pyramids, no Parthenon, no castles or cathedrals?' asked Mrs Allerton.

'Human beings matter more than stones. And the future is more important than the past.'

Signor Richetti, whose special interest was ancient ruins, argued with the young man about art and politics until the boat landed.

◆

After lunch, the passengers for the Second Cataract – including Monsieur Poirot, the Allertons, the young man and the Italian,

25

but not Jacqueline de Bellefort – caught the train from Cairo to Shellal. The Otterbournes would join the group there.

Poirot found that he was sitting with an older lady who had a very lined face, a stiff white collar, diamonds around her neck and an arrogant expression on her face. After a quick look at Poirot, she retired behind her American magazine. Now and then she raised her eyes and shouted an order at the shy young woman sitting opposite her:

'Cornelia, collect the coats.' 'When we arrive, look for my case. Under no circumstances let anyone else handle it.'

The train journey was very short and soon the passengers were on the *Karnak* with the Otterbournes. Most of the passengers had cabins on the same deck. At the front of this deck there was a public lounge with windows on all sides, where the passengers could sit and watch the river.

After checking his cabin, Poirot joined Rosalie Otterbourne on the deck.

'So now we journey into Nubia.* You are pleased, Mademoiselle?'

The girl took a deep breath. 'Yes. I feel that we're really getting away from things at last. Away from *people*. There's something about this country that makes me feel – evil. It reminds me that everything's so unfair. Look at some people's mothers – and look at mine. The only God is Sex …' She stopped. 'I shouldn't say such things, I suppose.'

'Why not say them – to me? Say them and then let them go.'

She smiled at Poirot. 'What an extraordinary man you are!' Then her faced changed again. 'Well, here are Mr and Mrs Doyle. I had no idea *they* were coming on this trip!'

Simon and Linnet Doyle looked relaxed and brilliantly happy, and held hands as the *Karnak* began its seven-day journey to the

---

* Nubia: a desert region and ancient nation in the Nile River valley

Second Cataract and back.

From behind them came a light laugh. Linnet turned her head in shock. Jacqueline de Bellefort was standing there. She seemed amused.

'Hello, Linnet! I didn't expect to find *you* here. I thought you said you were staying in Assuan for another ten days.'

Linnet and Simon moved to the other side of the boat. Simon looked wild with anger; their pleasure had gone. Without turning his head, Poirot heard bits of their conversation: ' ... turn back ... impossible ... Lin, we've got to go on with it now ... '

◆

In the early evening, Poirot stood alone in the public lounge. Suddenly, Linnet Doyle stood by his side. She looked nervous and worried, like a confused child.

'Monsieur Poirot, I'm afraid – I'm afraid of everything. The dark water, the wild rocks. I've never felt like this. Except for Simon, I'm surrounded by enemies.'

'But what is all this, Madame?'

'Perhaps it's nerves ... I just feel unsafe. Trapped! What's going to happen? How did she know we were coming on this boat?'

'She has brains, you know,' answered Poirot. 'With your money, why did you not hire a private boat?'

'We didn't expect this trouble. And Simon is sensitive about money. He wanted a honeymoon that *he* could pay for. I've got to educate him gradually about the finer things in life.' Then her mood changed. 'I must change my clothes. I'm sorry, Monsieur Poirot. I'm afraid I've been talking a lot of foolish nonsense.'

◆

In the dining-room, Mrs Allerton said to her son, 'I asked little Hercule Poirot to sit at our table.'

'Mother, you didn't!' Tim sounded annoyed. 'He'll be with

us day and night.'

Mrs Allerton looked upset. Tim was usually so good-tempered. Men were difficult to understand! 'I'm sorry, my dear. I thought it would amuse you. You love detective stories.'

As they sat down, Hercule Poirot crossed the room to their table. 'You really allow me, Madame, to join you?'

'Please sit down, Monsieur Poirot,' Mrs Allerton said, smiling. She noticed his quick look at Tim, who still seemed angry, so talked cheerfully to produce a more pleasant atmosphere. 'Here's the passenger list. Let's try and match names to people. We know Miss de Bellefort and the Otterbournes. And, of course, Mr and Mrs Doyle. I think Dr Bessner must be the fat German with the moustache. And Mr Fanthorp must be the very quiet young man. Quite a nice face, cautious and intelligent.'

'Yes,' agreed Poirot. 'I wonder what he is doing here.'

'I think Mr Ferguson must be the young man who hates the rich. And Mr Pennington is the American who Mrs Doyle calls Uncle Andrew. I can imagine him in an office on Wall Street – extremely rich, I think. Next – Monsieur Hercule Poirot, whose talents are being wasted on this trip. Can't you find a crime for Monsieur Poirot, Tim?'

But her well-intended conversation only seemed to annoy her son more, and she quickly continued, 'We know Mr Richetti from Elephantine Island. Then Miss Van Schuyler – the very ugly old American lady who thinks she is better than everybody. Who are the two women with her?'

Finally, Tim decided to join his mother's game. 'Miss Bowers, the thin one with glasses, is her secretary and nurse. The other one is Miss Robson, a poor relation who seems to be enjoying herself although Miss Van Schuyler treats her like a slave. I heard them talking in the lounge before dinner.'

◆

On his way to his cabin later that night, Hercule Poirot saw Jacqueline de Bellefort standing alone on the deck. The look of pain on her face stopped him. She looked sad now, not frightening in any way.

'Good night, Mademoiselle.'

'Good night, Monsieur Poirot.' She hesitated, then said, 'You were surprised to find me here, on this trip?'

'More sorry than surprised. You have chosen, Mademoiselle, the dangerous path. I doubt now if you could turn back if you chose to.'

'That is true, but one must follow one's star, wherever it leads.'

'Be careful, Mademoiselle, that it is not a false star.'

Back in his cabin, Poirot was falling asleep when he heard Simon Doyle's voice, repeating the same words he had used when the steamboat left Shellal: 'We've got to go on with it now ... '

'Yes,' thought Hercule Poirot. 'We have to go on with it now.' He was not happy.

♦

After a stop at Ez-Zebua the next day, the *Karnak* continued its journey towards Wadi Halfa. The scenery was less frightening and the mood of the passengers was more cheerful.

Linnet seemed almost light-hearted as she sat in the public lounge with her husband and Mr Pennington.

'I know it's your honeymoon, Linnet,' said Pennington, 'but there are just one or two things ... '

'Of course, Uncle Andrew.' Linnet at once became businesslike. 'My marriage has made a difference, of course.'

'Yes. I will need your signature on several documents.' Pennington looked round quickly. The only other people in the lounge were Mr Ferguson, drinking beer at a small table, Hercule Poirot, who was sitting near him, and Miss Van Schuyler, who was sitting in a corner reading a book on Egypt.

Pennington left and returned with a large pile of papers.

'Have I got to sign all these?' Linnet asked.

'I know it's not a good time, but I'd like to get your affairs in proper order.' He sorted through the papers and Simon yawned.

The door to the lounge opened and Mr Fanthorp came in. He looked round and then walked over to the windows and stood near Poirot, looking out at the pale blue water.

Pennington put a document in front of Linnet, who examined it carefully.

'You sign just there,' he said as he pointed to the space for her signature. 'It's not very important. You needn't read it.'

Simon yawned again. 'My dear girl, if you read everything, we'll be here until lunch-time and longer.'

'I *always* read everything carefully,' said Linnet. 'Father taught me to do that. There could be a careless mistake.'

Pennington gave a rather cold laugh.

'I've never read a legal document in my life,' said Simon, laughing. 'I sign where they tell me to sign.'

Suddenly, to everyone's surprise, the silent Mr Fanthorp spoke to Linnet. 'Excuse me, but I must say that I respect your businesslike attitude. It's admirable to read a document before you sign it.' Then, rather red in the face, he turned again to study the banks of the Nile.

'Er – thank you,' Linnet said, trying not to laugh.

Andrew Pennington looked seriously annoyed and gathered up the documents. 'Perhaps some other time would be better,' he said coldly. 'We mustn't miss enjoying the scenery.'

As they left, Cornelia Robson hurried in. Miss Bowers followed her calmly.

'Where have you been?' Miss Van Schuyler said crossly. 'Cornelia, I expect a little attention from you. Miss Bowers, give me my medicine and find me a chair outside on the deck.

Cornelia, bring my sewing.'

After the three women left, Mr Ferguson remarked to the almost empty room, 'I'd like to kill that woman.'

Poirot, who had noted everything that had happened in the room, asked with interest, 'She is a type you dislike?'

'Definitely. She's never worked. She just uses people. There are a lot of people on this boat that the world would be better without.'

'Really?'

'Yes. That girl in here just now, signing documents. She's one of the richest women in England – and has never done a day's work.'

'Who told you that she was so rich?' asked Poirot.

'A man who works with his hands and is proud of it.'

'Me, I work with my brain and am proud of it,' said Poirot.

'They ought to be shot, all of them!'

'What a fondness you have for violence!'

'You've got to destroy before you can build up.'

'It is certainly much easier, noisier and more exciting.'

'What do *you* do for a living?' the young man asked. 'Nothing at all, I expect. You probably call yourself a middleman.'

'I am not a middleman. I am a top man,' Hercule Poirot said rather arrogantly.

'What *are* you?'

'I am a detective,' said Hercule Poirot proudly.

'No! Are you here to protect that rich girl? Does she think she needs a stupid detective with her?'

'I have no connection with the Doyles,' said Poirot coldly. 'I am on holiday. And you? Are you not on holiday too?'

'I'm studying conditions,' Ferguson said mysteriously.

'Very interesting,' Poirot said to himself.

He left the public lounge and walked along the right-hand deck. As he reached the back of the steamboat, he almost walked into a woman with an excitable dark face. She was neatly dressed in a maid's uniform and was talking to a big, well-built man – perhaps one of the *Karnak*'s engineers. A look of alarm and guilt appeared on both their faces when they saw Poirot.

Then, as he continued his walk back along the left-hand side of the boat, a door opened and Mrs Otterbourne nearly fell into his arms.

'Dear Mr Poirot – so very sorry,' she apologized. 'The boat moves so much. Never really happy on the water ...'

Poirot gently took her arm. 'I will send your daughter to you, Madame. Return to your cabin. The water is too rough. You might be swept off the deck.'

Mrs Otterbourne hesitated and then went back into her cabin.

Poirot found Rosalie sitting between Mrs Allerton and Tim. She was chatting and laughing quite happily, but her face changed when Monsieur Poirot said, 'Your mother wants you, Mademoiselle.'

As Rosalie hurried to her mother's cabin, Mrs Allerton said, 'I think she's a very complicated girl – very unhappy.'

'Well, I suppose we've all got our private troubles,' Tim replied.

♦

That evening, Poirot noticed Mrs Allerton talking to Miss Van Schuyler. As he passed their chairs, Mrs Allerton closed one eye and opened it again. She was saying, 'Of course at Calfries Castle – the dear Prince ... '

Cornelia was listening happily to Dr Bessner as the German told her everything he had read in his guidebook about ancient Egypt.

Poirot also heard Tim Allerton say, 'It's a horrible world ... '

Rosalie Otterbourne answered, 'It's unfair; some people have everything.'

Poirot was glad that he was no longer young.

Chapter 3   Tragedy Strikes

The *Karnak*'s next stop was at Abu Simbel. It was a beautiful, warm day and everybody wanted to see the ancient temple.

Simon Doyle had a quiet word with Poirot. 'I'm so glad we came on this trip. Linnet's *faced* this business at last and we've agreed that we aren't going to let Jackie upset us any more. We're going to enjoy our honeymoon. That ought to show her.'

'Yes,' said Poirot thoughtfully.

Linnet came along the deck, smiling and looking beautiful as usual. She greeted Poirot coolly and then took her husband away. Poirot realized that his critical attitude had made him unpopular. Linnet expected to be admired for everything she was or did.

Soon the official guide led the group from the *Karnak* towards Abu Simbel. Poirot walked beside Andrew Pennington.

'Madame Doyle was telling me that you came over on the *Carmanic*. Did you meet some friends of mine who were on that ship – the Rushington Smiths?' asked Poirot.

'I don't remember the name. The boat was full and the weather was bad, so a lot of passengers rarely appeared.'

'But now the pleasant coincidence of running into Madame Doyle and her husband. You had no idea they were married?'

'No. Mrs Doyle had written, but I didn't receive the letter until after our unexpected meeting in Cairo,' explained Pennington.

'You have known her for many years, I understand?'

'Since she was a small child. Her father and I were great friends. A very fine man, Melhuish Ridgeway – and a very successful one.'

'His daughter will receive a very large fortune when her father dies, I understand. Ah, *pardon** – that is a private matter.'

Andrew Pennington seemed slightly amused. 'Oh, most

---

* *pardon*: French for 'sorry'

people know that Linnet is a very wealthy woman.'

'Will the recent fall in the stock market affect her fortune?'

Pennington hesitated but finally said, 'Yes, of course, to some degree. The financial situation for everyone is difficult these days.'

Inside the temple, Signor Richetti examined the painted walls and Dr Bessner read aloud to Cornelia from his guidebook. She listened with great attention until Miss Van Schuyler called for her. Poirot realized that someone was always either instructing the poor girl or giving her orders.

Simon said suddenly, 'Linnet, let's get out of here. I don't like these old figures. There's something frightening about them.'

Linnet laughed, but they walked into the sunlight. Then they sat against the side of the hill.

'How lovely the sun is,' thought Linnet. 'How warm – how safe ... how lovely to be me – me ... me ... Linnet ... '

Simon also looked content. What a fool he'd been to be worried that first night ... There was nothing to worry about ... Everything was all right ... After all, one could trust Jackie ...

Suddenly, there was a shout – people were running towards him waving their arms. Simon jumped to his feet and dragged Linnet with him. Not a minute too soon. An enormous rock crashed down past them. If Linnet had remained where she was, she would have been killed.

White-faced, Linnet and Simon held each other. Hercule Poirot and Tim Allerton ran up to them.

'*Ma foi!** Madame, that was close.'

They saw nothing when they looked up at the hill. But Poirot remembered seeing some people walking along the path at the top when they had first stepped on shore.

'She'll pay for this!' Simon said violently. Then he looked quickly at Tim Allerton and was silent.

* *Ma foi!*: a French expression of surprise

'Was it an accident?' wondered Tim aloud. 'Or did some fool push it?'

Linnet was very pale and found it difficult to speak. 'I think,' she said slowly, 'some fool must have pushed it.'

As they walked back to the *Karnak*, Simon stopped suddenly in surprise. Jacqueline de Bellefort was just coming off the boat.

'Good God!' Simon whispered. 'It *was* an accident, after all. I thought – I thought – '

'Good morning,' Jacqueline said, and walked towards the temple.

Poirot looked back at the beach. He could see Miss Van Schuyler and Miss Bowers, and there was Mrs Allerton with Mrs Otterbourne. He could not see the others.

♦

The next day, most of the passengers from the *Karnak* decided to visit the Second Cataract.

Hercule Poirot and Mrs Allerton walked slowly up the hill together. Mrs Allerton had learned to like the little man very much, although Tim was always trying to keep her away from him. She found herself suddenly telling him about her dislike of Joanna Southwood.

Tim was chatting to Rosalie Otterbourne about his bad luck in life: poor health, but not bad enough to be interesting, very little money, nothing much to do.

Rosalie interrupted, 'But you have your mother! She looks lovely – so calm – but amusing, too.'

Tim was surprised and pleased. 'Mother? She's wonderful, isn't she? It's nice of you to see it.' He was embarrassed that he couldn't say anything nice about *her* mother.

Miss Van Schuyler had stayed on the boat. She was too old for the climb up to the Second Cataract. She complained about Cornelia to Miss Bowers.

'She rushed away without a word to me, and I saw her talking to that very unpleasant young man, Ferguson.'

Miss Bowers looked at the group as they walked down the hill. 'Miss Robson is with Dr Bessner now.'

Miss Van Schuyler was pleased with this arrangement. She had learned that Dr Bessner was a well-known, fashionable doctor in Europe. She decided to be polite to him in case she needed his professional services before the journey was over.

When the group returned to the *Karnak* Linnet cried, 'A telegram for me. How nice!' She seized it from the board and opened it.

'I don't understand – potatoes, beans, onions – what does it mean, Simon?'

Suddenly, an angry voice said, 'Excuse me, that telegram is for me,' and Signor Richetti took it rudely from her hand.

'I am so sorry, Signor Richetti. You see, my name was Ridgeway before I married, so … '

She smiled at Signor Richetti, but he did not excuse her mistake just because she was pretty.

'Names should be read carefully,' he said coldly.

Linnet turned away. 'These Italians are so rude,' she said angrily to Simon. The two of them went on shore alone.

Poirot, watching from the deck, turned to see Jacqueline de Bellefort beside him. Instead of looking amused or evil, she looked ill, as if a fire was burning inside her.

'They don't care any more. I can't hurt them. You were right. I ought not to have come, but I can't go back. I will not allow them to be happy together. I'd rather kill him … '

She turned suddenly and hurried away.

Poirot, staring after her, felt a hand on his shoulder. It was an old friend, Colonel Race, a man who travelled round the world solving important cases for the British government. He and Poirot had met a year previously, at a dinner party in London that had ended with the death of their host.

'Your friend seems a bit upset, Monsieur Poirot.'

'Colonel Race! What are you doing here?'

'I'm on the return journey to Shellal with you. I'm interested in one of the *Karnak*'s passengers, but unfortunately I don't know which one,' explained Colonel Race rather mysteriously. 'There's been a lot of political trouble out here – violence, murders. Our spies have told us that the cleverest of the leaders – the brains – is on this boat, but we don't have his name or description. Have you got any ideas?'

'An idea, but nothing more than that,' Poirot said thoughtfully.

Race knew that Poirot never spoke unless he was sure.

Poirot rubbed his nose and said unhappily, 'There is something else happening on this boat that is causing me much concern.'

'Tell me about it,' Race said with interest.

'Think about this,' said Poirot. 'A has wronged B. B desires revenge and threatens A. Both women are on this boat.'

'Don't worry,' said Race. 'People – especially women – who talk about what they are going to do don't usually do it. Anything else?'

'Yesterday A had a very close escape from death, the kind of death that might conveniently be called an accident.'

'Arranged by B?'

'No, that is the point. B did not do it. It was not possible.'

'Then it *was* an accident. Coincidences do happen.'

'I suppose so,' agreed Poirot, 'but I do not like such accidents.'

'Is A a particularly unpleasant person?' asked Race.

'Absolutely not. A is a charming, rich and beautiful young lady. And if I am right, and I am constantly in the habit of being right, then there is a matter for serious concern. And now *you* tell me there is a man on the *Karnak* who kills.'

'He doesn't usually kill charming young ladies.'

'Today I advised A, Madame Doyle, to take another route and not to return on this boat,' said Poirot. 'But she and her husband would not agree. I pray to heaven that we may arrive at Shellal without disaster – but I, Hercule Poirot, I am afraid.'

♦

On the following evening the *Karnak* stopped at Abu Simbel, giving the passengers the opportunity for a second visit to the temple.

'There's so much to see!' Cornelia Robson said excitedly to Mr Ferguson. 'I wish Dr Bessner was here. He'd explain it all to me.'

'How can you like that boring old fool? And that old woman. She treats you like a dog. You're as good as they are!'

'But I'm not,' protested Cornelia. 'Cousin Marie is very cultured, and ...'

'Cultured! That word makes me sick.' Ferguson paused. 'Don't you realize – as an American – that everyone is born free and equal?'

'Of course people aren't equal,' said Cornelia calmly. 'I'm not beautiful and rich like Mrs Doyle.'

'Mrs Doyle!' shouted Ferguson. 'She's the sort of woman who ought to be shot as an example.'

There was an uncomfortable silence. But before they returned to the *Karnak*, Ferguson said, 'You're the nicest person on the boat. Remember that.'

Feeling unusually pleased, Cornelia hurried into the public lounge to find Miss Van Schuyler.

The old lady looked at her watch. 'You've been a long time!' she said crossly. 'And what have you done with my velvet shawl? I had it in here after dinner. It was on that chair.'

'I can't see it anywhere, Cousin Marie,' said Cornelia after a quick search.

Miss Van Schuyler left the room in a bad temper, with Cornelia and Miss Bowers following behind.

Most of the other passengers had also gone to bed early. The Doyles remained in the lounge, playing cards with Pennington and Colonel Race at a table in a corner. Fanthorp was reading a book. The only other passenger in the lounge was Hercule Poirot, who could not stop yawning. He, too, decided on an early night.

As he walked sleepily towards his cabin, Poirot met Jacqueline hurrying along the deck.

'You look sleepy, Monsieur Poirot.'

'*Mais oui** – I can hardly keep my eyes open,' said Poirot. 'It has been a very hot day – no wind at all.'

'Yes,' Jacqueline said thoughtfully. 'It's been the sort of day when things – break! When one can't go on … '

She seemed tense and nervous, but she relaxed when she said good night. Her eyes met his, just for a moment. Poirot remembered that look the next day. Had there been a cry for help?

He continued to his cabin.

After dealing with Miss Van Schuyler's many needs, Cornelia decided that she was not sleepy and returned to the public lounge. She looked up from her sewing when the door opened and Jacqueline de Bellefort came in. Jacqueline pressed the bell for a waiter, then sat down with Cornelia.

'A lovely night,' Jacqueline commented. 'A real honeymoon night, isn't it?' Her eyes rested on Linnet Doyle.

When the waiter arrived, Jacqueline ordered a large drink. Simon looked up from his cards with a faint line of worry on his forehead.

When her drink came, Jacqueline picked it up and said, 'Well, here's to crime.' She finished it quickly and ordered another.

* *mais oui*: a French expression of agreement

Again, Simon looked across the room at her. He seemed to lose his concentration in the card game, and soon Linnet and Colonel Race stood up to leave

'Coming, Simon?' asked Linnet.

'Not yet. I think I'll have a drink first.'

Pennington finished his drink and left. Cornelia began to gather up her sewing.

'Please don't go to bed, Miss Robson,' said Jacqueline. 'Don't leave me. We girls must support each other.'

Cornelia sat down again.

Jacqueline's second drink arrived, and she began to sing quietly: *'He was her man and he did her wrong ... '*

Mr Fanthorp turned a page of his book. Simon Doyle picked up a magazine.

'Really, I think I'll go to bed,' said Cornelia. 'It's very late.'

'I forbid you to go,' Jacqueline replied. 'Tell me about yourself.'

Cornelia was confused. Obviously Jacqueline was drinking too much. But there was something else ... Jacqueline was talking to her − was looking at her − but it seemed that the words she said were meant for someone else. But Cornelia did as requested and began telling Jacqueline every detail of her life. Again, she sensed that Jacqueline was listening to something else − or perhaps *for* something else?

Then Jacqueline turned her head and spoke to Simon Doyle: 'Ring the bell, Simon. I want another drink.'

'It's late − and you've had enough to drink, Jackie.'

Jacqueline laughed. 'Simon's afraid I'm going to tell you the story of *my* life,' she said to Cornelia. 'He treated me rather badly, didn't you, Simon?'

Cornelia was deeply embarrassed, but also pleasantly excited. What an angry look Simon Doyle had on his face.

'You're drunk,' he said. 'You're making a fool of yourself.'

Cornelia began to stand up. 'I really must – it's so late –'

'No, stay and listen. He's embarrassed. He wants me to behave "well", don't you, Simon? But I'm going to talk – a lot.'

Jim Fanthorp carefully shut his book, yawned, looked at his watch and left the room. A very British performance.

Jacqueline stared at Simon. 'I told you,' she said, 'that I'd kill you before I'd let you go to another woman … You don't think I meant that? *You're wrong.* I've only been – waiting. You're mine. Do you hear?'

Simon remained silent. Jacqueline reached into in her handbag, and then leant forward with something shiny in her hand.

'I'll shoot you like a dog – like the dirty dog you are … '

Simon jumped to his feet, but at the same moment Jacqueline fired the gun.

Simon fell, twisted across a chair … Cornelia screamed and rushed to the door. Jim Fanthorp was outside on the deck.

'Mr Fanthorp!' Cornelia cried. 'Oh! She's shot him!'

Simon Doyle still lay across the chair. Jacqueline stood staring at the blood on his trouser leg, where he was holding a handkerchief to the wound.

'I didn't mean … Oh, my God, I didn't really mean … '

The pistol dropped from her nervous fingers to the floor. She kicked it away and it slid under one of the sofas.

Simon whispered: 'Fanthorp – there's someone coming … Say it's all right – an accident – something.'

Fanthorp spoke quickly to the waiter who was hurrying through the door: 'All right – everything's all right. Just a bit of fun.' The Nubian left again.

Jacqueline began crying uncontrollably. 'Oh, God, I want to die … Oh, what have I done – what have I done?'

Simon's face was twisted with pain. 'Take her to her cabin, Fanthorp. Miss Robson, get that hospital nurse of yours to look after her. Don't leave her alone. Then bring old Bessner here.

And please don't let any news of this get to my wife.'

Fanthorp and Cornelia soon had Jacqueline back in her cabin, but she would not calm down. 'I'll kill myself ... Oh, Simon – Simon!'

Fanthorp said to Cornelia, 'Find Miss Bowers. I'll stay with her.'

'Simon could bleed to death!' Jacqueline cried. 'I must help him. Let me go!'

Fanthorp held her by her shoulders. 'Quietly – quietly. You must stay here. He'll be all right.'

Very soon Cornelia returned with Miss Bowers, who immediately took charge of the situation.

Some minutes later, Fanthorp managed to wake the heavily sleeping Dr Bessner and the two men hurried back to the lounge. Simon, grey-faced, had his head against an open window, breathing in the cool night air. The handkerchief now lay in a pool of blood on the floor.

The doctor examined Simon's leg and said, 'Yes, it is bad ... The bone is broken. And he has lost a lot of blood. Mr Fanthorp, you and I must carry him to my cabin. He cannot walk.'

There, Dr Bessner took care of Simon's bullet wound and then gave him something to help him sleep.

'What should we do about your wife?' he asked.

Simon said weakly, 'She needn't know until morning. And I – you mustn't blame Jackie. I treated her badly. She didn't know what she was doing .... Someone ought to stay with her. She might hurt herself – '

'It's all right, Mr Doyle,' said Fanthorp. 'Miss Bowers is going to stay with her all night.'

Simon relaxed, then opened his eyes again. 'Fanthorp?' he called. 'The pistol ... ought not to leave it lying about.'

Fanthorp understood. 'Quite right. I'll go and get it now.'

Three minutes later, he was back at Bessner's cabin. He spoke quietly to the doctor.

'I can't find that pistol. I saw the girl drop it and kick it under a sofa, but it isn't there now.'

They stared at each other, puzzled and rather alarmed.

♦

The next morning, Hercule Poirot was shaving when Colonel Race hurried into his cabin.

'Your feeling was correct. It's happened,' Race began. 'Linnet Doyle's dead – shot through the head last night.'

Poirot was silent for a minute. Two memories came back to him very clearly. First, a girl in a garden in Assuan saying, 'There are moments when I want to hurt her – to put my pistol against her head and shoot her – ' And the same voice saying more recently, 'Yes ... it's been the sort of day when things – break! When one can't go on ... ' Why had he not answered her cry for help? He had been blind, deaf, stupid with his need for sleep ...

The two men went to Linnet's cabin, where they found Dr Bessner examining the body.

'What can you tell us, Doctor, about this business?' asked Race.

'The gun was held against her head. The bullet entered just above the ear. The skin is burned and black around the bullet hole. The murderer shot her as she lay sleeping.'

'*Non!*'* Poirot cried out. This description did not fit with his picture of Jacqueline de Bellefort. She would not act in this way.

Then Poirot looked up and saw a big, shaky letter J written in a brownish-red colour on the white wall next to Linnet's bed. He lifted the dead girl's right hand and found the same brownish-red colour on one of her fingers.

* *non*: French for 'no'

43

'What do you think of that?' asked Race.

'It is very simple, is it not? Madame Doyle is dying; she wishes to name her killer, and so she writes with her finger, using her own blood, the first letter of her murderer's name. It has often been done in crime novels. It makes me think that our murderer is – old-fashioned!'

'What does J stand for?' asked Race.

Poirot answered immediately. 'J is for Jacqueline de Bellefort, a young lady who has a pistol and who told me less than a week ago that she would like to shoot Madame Doyle.'

Bessner said, 'We will have to remove the bullet to be certain about the gun.'

'What about the time of death?' asked Race.

'She has been dead certainly for six hours and probably not longer than eight. So she was murdered between midnight and two o'clock in the morning.'

'Where is her husband?' asked Race.

'At the moment he is sleeping in my cabin,' said Dr Bessner. 'I see from your surprise that you have not been told that Mr Doyle was shot last night in the public lounge.'

'Shot? By whom?'

'By the young lady, Jacqueline de Bellefort. The bone in his leg is badly broken. He needs hospital treatment.'

'The captain has given us an office,' Race said. 'Our first job is to get all the facts.'

Chapter 4 Everyone is a Suspect

In the office, Colonel Race and Poirot began their enquiry.

First, they listened to Dr Bessner's thorough report of the previous night.

Race said, 'It seems clear enough. The girl got excited, helped

44

by a drink or two, and finally shot Simon Doyle. Then she went along to Linnet Doyle's cabin and shot her too.'

'No, I do not think that was *possible*,' Bessner interrupted. 'First, she was never alone after she shot Mr Doyle. And second, why would she write the first letter of her own name on the wall?'

'It would not be her style,' agreed Poirot. 'But perhaps someone else wanted to direct our attention to her? Who discovered the crime?'

'Mrs Doyle's maid, Louise Bourget. She went to call Mrs Doyle as usual, found her dead, came out of the cabin and fainted. The captain was called and then he came to me,' reported Race. 'Doyle's got to be told. You say he's asleep still?'

'Yes, in my cabin,' Bessner said. 'I gave him a strong sleeping drug last night.'

'Thank you, Doctor,' said Race. 'I don't think we need to keep you longer. We'll begin to question the other passengers.'

As they waited for Fanthorp and Miss Robson, witnesses to what had happened to Simon Doyle, Race said, 'This is bad. Have you any ideas about this murder?'

'My ideas are not in good order,' Poirot replied. 'We know, you see, that this girl wanted to kill Linnet Doyle.'

'But would she do it in this way?' asked Race. 'Could she?'

'She would have the brains for this murder, and the motive. But I doubt if, physically, she could face committing the *act* … '

'I see,' agreed Race. 'And remember, Bessner also said it was physically impossible.'

'I hope that is true,' Poirot said and paused. 'I shall be glad if it is, because I am sympathetic to that little one.'

The door opened. Fanthorp and Cornelia Robson entered.

Race began, 'I said good night to Mrs Doyle at her cabin door at eleven twenty. Who remained in the public lounge after she left?'

Fanthorp answered, 'Doyle was there. And Miss de Bellefort.

Myself and Miss Robson.'

'That's right,' agreed Cornelia. 'Mr Pennington went to bed a few minutes after Mrs Doyle.'

'So what was everyone doing after Pennington left?'

'Mr Fanthorp was reading a book. I'd got some sewing, Miss de Bellefort was – she was – '

'Drinking quite heavily.' Mr Fanthorp helped her.

'And she was talking to me, but I think most of her comments were meant for Mr Doyle,' said Cornelia. 'He was getting angry, but he kept quiet. I think he hoped she would calm down, but she didn't, and she wouldn't let me leave the lounge. I was getting very uncomfortable with the situation. Then Mr Fanthorp left.'

'It was a little embarrassing, so I left quietly,' said Fanthorp.

'Then she pulled out a pistol,' continued Cornelia, 'and Mr Doyle jumped up to try and take it from her, and it shot him in the leg; and then she began to cry – and I was frightened to death and ran out after Mr Fanthorp. Mr Doyle wanted to keep everything quiet, so we took Jacqueline to her cabin, and Mr Fanthorp stayed with her while I got Miss Bowers.'

'What time was this?' Race asked.

Cornelia hesitated, but Fanthorp said, 'It was about twenty minutes past twelve. I know it was actually half past twelve when I finally got to my cabin.'

'Now let me be quite sure on one or two points,' said Poirot. 'After Madame Doyle left the lounge, did any of the four of you leave it?'

Fanthorp answered immediately, 'No. I'm positive. Neither Doyle, Miss de Bellefort, Miss Robson, nor myself left the lounge.'

'So Mademoiselle de Bellefort did not leave the lounge and shoot Madame Doyle before twenty past twelve. Mademoiselle Robson, when you went to fetch Mademoiselle Bowers, was

Jacqueline de Bellefort alone in her cabin at any time?'

'No. Mr Fanthorp stayed with her.'

'She has a perfect alibi. But Monsieur Doyle, you say, was very anxious that she should not be left alone. Was he afraid, do you think, that she was considering another foolish act?'

'That's my opinion,' said Fanthorp. 'He was afraid she might even try to kill herself. She kept saying she would be better dead.'

Cornelia said shyly, 'Mr Doyle said it was all his fault – that he'd treated her badly. He spoke quite nicely about her.'

Poirot looked thoughtful. 'Now what happened to that pistol? Tell me exactly what happened.'

'Miss de Bellefort let the gun fall. Then she kicked it away and it went under a sofa,' Fanthorp continued, explaining how he had gone back to search for it, but had not been able to find it.

'So we arrive at this point. When Mademoiselle de Bellefort left the lounge, the pistol was under the sofa. After that, she had no opportunity to return to the lounge for it. What time was it, Monsieur Fanthorp, when you went back to look for it?'

'Just before half past twelve – about five minutes after Dr Bessner and I carried Doyle out of the lounge.'

'In those few minutes someone – *not* Mademoiselle de Bellefort – took that pistol from under the sofa. It seems very probable that the person who removed it was the murderer of Madame Doyle. And also that this person had heard or seen Mademoiselle de Bellefort shoot Doyle.'

'I don't see how you can know that,' objected Fanthorp.

'You have told us that the pistol was hidden under the sofa. Therefore it is hardly possible that it was discovered by *accident*. It was taken by someone who knew it was there,' explained Poirot.

Fanthorp shook his head. 'I saw nobody when I went out on the deck just before Miss de Bellefort shot Doyle.'

'But you were outside on the right side of the boat. From that position one cannot see someone on the opposite side looking through the glass door of the public lounge. Did anyone except the waiter hear the shot?' Poirot asked.

'No. The windows and doors were closed because Miss Van Schuyler felt cold earlier in the evening,' answered Fanthorp.

Race added, 'No one seems to have heard the other shot – the shot that killed Mrs Doyle.'

'For the moment, let us concentrate on the first shooting,' Poirot said. 'We must speak to Mademoiselle Bowers. But first, before we finish here, may we have a little information about the two of you?'

Fanthorp and Miss Robson gave their full names, addresses and professions. Then Poirot asked Fanthorp, 'And your reasons for visiting this country?'

'Er – pleasure – a holiday,' Fanthorp answered after a pause.

'Very well, Monsieur Fanthorp. A final question: Did you hear anything at all after you went to your cabin?'

Fanthorp thought for a moment. 'I went to bed very quickly. I *think* I heard something as I was falling asleep – a splash. Nothing else.'

'Did the splash seem close? What time was it?'

'I was half asleep, but I think it was about one o'clock. I don't know how close it was.'

'Thank you.' Poirot turned to Cornelia. 'Now, Mademoiselle Robson. What did you do after helping Dr Bessner with Monsieur Doyle's leg?'

'I went to my cabin, the one next to Miss de Bellefort. The boat's against the bank on my side, so I didn't hear any splashes.'

Poirot thanked Fanthorp and Cornelia, and they left.

'According to three witnesses, Jacqueline de Bellefort did not pick up the pistol after she kicked it under the sofa,' said Race.

Miss Bowers was next in the office. After the usual questions, Poirot asked, 'How is Mademoiselle Van Schuyler's health?'

'There's nothing seriously wrong with her,' replied Miss Bowers. 'She's just old. She likes plenty of attention and can pay for it.'

'Please tell us about Mademoiselle de Bellefort last night.'

'Miss Robson came for me and told me what had happened. Miss de Bellefort had drunk a large amount of alcohol. She was excited and upset. I gave her a drug to calm her, and I sat with her.'

'Did either of you leave her cabin at any time?'

'No. I was in the cabin with her until early this morning. I am absolutely sure that she didn't leave.'

After the nurse went out, the two men looked at each other. Jacqueline de Bellefort was definitely not the murderer. So who had shot Linnet Doyle?

'Someone took the pistol, thinking that Jacqueline de Bellefort would be accused of the murder,' said Race. 'But that person – the real murderer – did not know that Miss Bowers would be with Miss de Bellefort all night. Add this to the fact that someone – again *not* Miss de Bellefort – had already attempted to kill Linnet Doyle at the temple. Who was that person?'

Poirot said, 'Doyle, the Allertons, Mademoiselle Van Schuyler and Mademoiselle Bowers were within my sight at the temple. They did not push the rock, but there are others to consider.'

Their discussion was interrupted by the entrance of Jacqueline de Bellefort. Race left her alone with Poirot.

'I didn't do it,' she said in the voice of a frightened child. 'Oh, please believe me. It's awful.'

Poirot gently touched her shoulder. 'Do not be upset. We know that you did not kill Madame Doyle. It is proved, *mon enfant*.'*

'But who did?' Jacqueline asked tearfully.

---

* *mon enfant*: French for 'my child'

'That,' said Poirot, 'is the question we are asking ourselves. You cannot help us, my child?'

Jacqueline shook her head. 'I don't know,' she said. 'I can't think of anyone who wanted her dead ... except me.'

She looked down, nervously twisting her fingers, and suddenly cried out, 'Death's horrible – horrible! I – hate the thought of it.'

Poirot said, 'Yes. It is not pleasant, is it, to think that someone is at this moment celebrating his or her success.'

'Please, stop!' Jacqueline shouted. Then in a quiet voice: 'I wanted her dead – and she *is* dead – and she died – just like I said.'

'Yes, Mademoiselle. She was shot through the head.'

'Then I was right, that night at the Cataract Hotel. There *was* someone listening.'

'Ah! I wondered if you would remember that evening. It is too much of a coincidence that Madame Doyle was killed in just the way you described.'

Jacqueline's voice shook. 'That man that night – who was he?'

Poirot was silent for a minute or two, then said, 'You are sure it was a man, Mademoiselle?'

Jacqueline looked at him in surprise and said slowly, 'I *thought* it was a man ... but it was really just a – a figure – a shadow ... '

The door opened and Dr Bessner appeared.

'Will you come and speak with Mr Doyle, please, Monsieur Poirot? He would like to see you.'

Jacqueline jumped up. She caught Bessner by the arm.

'Is he all right? He's not going to die?' she cried.

'Who said anything about dying? We will get him to hospital for proper treatment.'

The girl's face relaxed and she sat down again while Poirot hurried off to Bessner's cabin to speak to Doyle.

Poirot stood in the doorway and examined Doyle's face, which showed pain, shock, but also child-like confusion.

Simon whispered, 'Please come in. I simply can't believe that Linnet is dead. But Jackie didn't do it. She wouldn't murder someone in cold blood.'

Poirot said gently, 'Mademoiselle de Bellefort did not shoot your wife. But who else wanted to kill her?'

Simon shook his head. 'Apart from Jackie, there's nobody. Of course, there's Windlesham. She refused him and married me, but he's in Canada now. And there's old Sir George Wode, who was unhappy about selling his house and seeing Linnet make all those changes, but he's in London.'

'Monsieur Doyle,' Poirot said seriously, 'I had a conversation with Madame, your wife, on the first day on the *Karnak*. She said she felt afraid, unsafe. She felt that *everyone* around her was an enemy.'

'We were both upset at finding Jackie on the boat.'

'That is understandable, but it does not quite explain Madame Doyle's feelings,' continued Poirot.

'Well, there was a name on the passenger list that upset her. She said it was someone whose father had done business with her father and had lost everything. Linnet said, "It's awful when people hate you without even knowing you".'

'You are quite sure that she did not mention this man's name?'

'I didn't really pay much attention,' Simon Doyle said.

Bessner said dryly, 'I can have a guess. I heard that young man Ferguson criticize Mrs Doyle once or twice.'

'We must not form theories until we talk to everyone,' advised Poirot. 'We ought to interview the maid first. Can we do that here? Monsieur Doyle's presence might be helpful.'

'Yes, that's a good idea,' said Simon.

'Had she been with your wife long?'

'Just a couple of months, that's all.'

'Only a couple of months? And had Madame any valuable jewellery?'

'There were her pearls,' said Simon. 'She once told me they were worth about fifty thousand pounds. My God, do you think those pearls ...?'

'Robbery is a possible but unlikely motive. Let us see the maid.'

Louise Bourget was the attractive, dark-haired woman who Poirot had noticed one day, but now she looked sad and frightened.

'When did you last see Madame Doyle alive?'

'Last night, Monsieur. I helped her to undress, and then I went to my cabin on the deck below some time after eleven.'

'Did you see or hear anything unusual last night?' asked Poirot.

'My cabin is on the other side of the boat, on the deck below. Naturally, if I had been unable to sleep and if I had climbed the stairs, *then* perhaps I would have seen this killer enter or leave Madame's cabin, but – what can I say?'

'My good girl,' Simon said roughly, 'I'll look after you. Nobody's accusing you of anything.'

'And you know of no one on this boat who would want to hurt Madame Doyle?' asked Poirot.

The maid's answer surprised everyone. 'Yes, that I do know. There was Mademoiselle de Bellefort, of course, but there was also someone else who disliked Madame.'

'Good lord!' Simon cried. 'What's all this?'

Louise went on excitedly, 'Yes, yes, yes, it is as I say! Madame's former maid, Marie, was engaged to marry one of the engineers on this boat. But Madame Doyle discovered that this man, Fleetwood, already had a wife in Egypt. Marie ended the engagement, but Fleetwood was very angry. When he found out that Madame was on this boat, he told me that she had ruined his life and he would like to kill her!'

Poirot turned to Simon. 'Had you any idea of this?'

'None, and I doubt if Linnet even knew that the man was on the boat. She had probably forgotten all about the affair.'

Poirot turned sharply to the maid. 'Did you say anything about Fleetwood to Madame Doyle?'

'No, Monsieur, of course not.'

'And do you know anything about Madame's pearls?'

'Her pearls?' Louise's eyes opened wide. 'She was wearing them last night. She put them on the table beside her bed, as always.'

'And did you see them this morning?' asked the detective.

'*Mon Dieu!** I did not even look.'

'You did not look,' said Poirot. 'But I – I have eyes which notice, and there were no pearls on the bedside table this morning.'

After searching Linnet Doyle's cabin and failing to find her pearls, Poirot and Colonel Race returned to their office.

'What do we know now?' asked Race.

'Aha! I see you have had an idea, my friend,' Poirot answered.

'Yes. I was thinking about the sound that Fanthorp mentioned. It's possible that after the murder, the killer threw the pistol into the water. It was not in Mrs Doyle's cabin.'

'Ah, the logical place for the pistol is in Mademoiselle de Bellefort's cabin, but perhaps it has not yet been put there.'

'Yes, I see,' said Race thoughtfully. 'But now there are the missing pearls and the man Fleetwood. It seems obvious that the pearls have been stolen.'

'But it was an odd moment to choose for a robbery, was it not? And why would a thief kill a sleeping woman? It is unsatisfactory ... You know, I have a little idea about those pearls – but – no – it is impossible. Because if my idea was right, the pearls would be in Madame Doyle's cabin. Tell me, what did you think of the maid?'

* *Mon Dieu!*: French for 'My God!'

'I wondered,' said Race slowly, 'if she knew more than she said.'

'Ah, you too had that impression? I would not trust her.'

'Do you think she had something to do with the murder?'

'The theft of the pearls is more probable – maids have been known to be members of gangs that steal jewellery. But that explanation does not quite satisfy me. My other idea *ought* to be right, but – ' Poirot stopped.

'What about the man Fleetwood?' asked Race.

'He may give us our solution,' said Poirot. 'He had a motive for revenge, and it is possible that he heard the scene between Mademoiselle de Bellefort and Monsieur Doyle and removed the pistol from the public lounge without anyone noticing. But that solution seems too simple, too easy.'

'Any other possibilities?' asked Race.

'Plenty, my friend. There is, for example, the American trustee, Pennington. Did he accidentally meet Linnet and Simon Doyle? And accidentally have a number of papers for Linnet to sign? Did he hope that she would sign them without reading them? Had he used her money for his own business? I know that is the way in all detective novels – but it happens, my friend, *it happens.*'

'I don't doubt it,' said Race.

'But Madame Doyle wanted to read each paper before signing. And then her husband made an important remark.'

'What was that?'

'He says – "I sign where they tell me to sign." Pennington saw the importance of that. If the wife died, the new husband would have her fortune, and he would sign anything. *Mon cher Colonel,** I saw the thought pass through Pennington's head.'

'But you've no proof,' said Race dryly.

---

* *mon cher Colonel*: French for 'my dear Colonel'

'I have not.'

'Might young Ferguson be the one whose father was ruined by old Ridgeway? Or there's the man *I'm* looking for – *he's* a killer, but it's unlikely that he knew Mrs Doyle.'

Their discussion was interrupted by a knock on the door and Fleetwood, a big, angry-looking man, entered the room.

'You wanted to see me?' he asked rather rudely.

'We did,' said Race. 'You probably know that a murder was committed on this boat last night? And I believe you had reason to feel anger against the woman who was killed.'

A look of alarm appeared in Fleetwood's eyes. 'Who told you that?' he shouted. 'That lying French girl!'

'You were going to marry the girl Marie, but Miss Ridgeway discovered you were a married man already.'

'What business was it of hers? My wife returned to Egypt – I hadn't seen her for more than six years. Marie wouldn't know about her if that grand lady hadn't involved herself in our business. I was angry, but I'm not a murderer. I was asleep in my cabin all night – and the man I share it with was too.'

After Fleetwood left, Race and Poirot agreed that he was probably telling the truth, but they would check his alibi.

'I, too, slept all night,' remarked Poirot. 'Very deeply. I heard nothing at all.'

'Let's hope we have more luck with the people on the right side of the boat,' Race said as Mrs Allerton arrived, looking quite upset.

'It's too horrible,' she said. 'That lovely creature – dead. Monsieur Poirot, I'm glad *you* are on board.'

'If you please, a few questions. You went to bed when?'

'Tim and I went to our cabins early. I went to bed just after half past ten. I fell asleep immediately.'

'And did you hear anything during the night?'

Mrs Allerton concentrated. 'Yes, I think I heard a splash and someone running. I had the idea that someone had fallen in, but it was like a dream – and then I woke up and listened, and everything was quite quiet.'

'Had you actually met Madame Doyle before?' asked Poirot.

'No. Tim had met her, and I'd heard a lot about her through our cousin, Joanna Southwood.'

'One more question, Madame, if you will pardon me for asking.'

Mrs Allerton smiled faintly. 'Of course.'

'Did you or your family ever suffer any financial loss as a result of the business affairs of Madame Doyle's father, Melhuish Ridgeway?'

Mrs Allerton looked very surprised. 'Oh, no! We don't have much, but we still have the money my husband left for us.'

Tim Allerton, too, had gone to bed early and had heard somebody running along the deck and a splash.

'A splash? Was it perhaps a shot?' asked Poirot.

'Perhaps it was a shot, or a cork from a bottle. There were loud voices, and I thought someone was having a party. But then everything went quiet and I fell asleep again.'

Miss Van Schuyler, who entered the room with an almost poisonous expression of displeasure, was next to be interviewed. Linnet Doyle's cabin lay between Simon Doyle's and hers.

'I do not wish to be involved in any way in this very unpleasant affair,' she said.

Poirot said politely, 'Of course, Mademoiselle. We wish to free you from unpleasantness as quickly as possible. Just a few questions. First, you went to bed last night – at what time?'

'Ten o'clock is my usual time. Last night I went later because Cornelia Robson, very rudely, kept me waiting.'

'*Très bien.** Now what did you hear after you were in bed?'

---

* *très bien*: French for 'very well'

'I was awakened by Mrs Doyle's rather loud maid, who said, "*Bonne nuit, Madame*".* Then I went to sleep again until I heard someone in Mrs Doyle's cabin next door. Then someone outside on the deck, and then a splash.'

'You have no idea what time this was?'

'I can tell you the time exactly. I looked at my little clock and it was ten minutes past one. And I know who was responsible for the splash because I got up and looked out.'

Colonel Race sat up. 'You know?'

'Certainly. I saw Miss Otterbourne leaning over the side of the boat. She had just dropped something into the water. I saw her face very clearly.'

'And what did her face look like, Mademoiselle?'

'She was very upset – too emotional to see me. Then she walked away and I returned to bed.'

There was a knock at the door and the captain entered. He carried something in his hand.

'We've got it, Colonel,' he said with excitement.

Race took the package and slowly unwrapped several layers of wet velvet cloth. Out of it fell a cheap handkerchief with a faint pink stain on it. Inside was a small pearl-handled pistol.

'I was right,' Race said to Poirot. 'It *was* thrown into the water. Is it the pistol you saw at the Cataract Hotel that night?'

Poirot examined the gun carefully, then he said quietly, 'Yes – here are the initials JB.'

Race opened the pistol and said, 'Two bullets fired. There seems no doubt that this is the murder weapon.'

'And what about my shawl?' demanded Miss Van Schuyler. 'I was asking everyone if they had seen it last night.'

'This is yours?' asked Race, picking up the wet cloth. 'The murderer wrapped it round the pistol to soften the noise of the

* *Bonne nuit, Madame.* French for 'Good night, Madam'.

57

shot. You can see the burn marks from the bullet.'

'Shocking!' said Miss Van Schuyler crossly.

'Miss Van Schuyler, how well did you know Mrs Doyle?'

'I had never met her before. Her family had money, but they were nobodies – not our type of people.'

When the old woman left, the two men looked at each other.

'Can we believe her story?' asked Race.

'It does not make sense!' Poirot cried. 'Someone shot Linnet Doyle and wrote the letter J on the wall. We would expect that person to leave the pistol in Madame Doyle's cabin for someone to find. Therefore, why was the pistol thrown into the water? Why, my friend, why? The series of events is *impossible*. Something is wrong.'

'Shall we talk to Rosalie Otterbourne next?' Race suggested.

When she arrived, the girl looked unwilling, but not nervous.

'You know that we are making enquiries about Mrs Doyle's death. Will you tell me what you did last night?' Race asked.

'Mother and I went to bed early – before eleven. We heard voices outside Dr Bessner's cabin, but nothing else.'

'Did you leave your cabin at all last night?'

'No, definitely not.'

'Miss Van Schuyler says that she saw you throwing something into the water at ten minutes past one.'

'It's a complete lie. Did she see anything else?'

'No, but she heard someone moving about in Madame Doyle's cabin.'

Rosalie Otterbourne now looked extremely pale.

'Do you still insist that you threw nothing into the water, Mademoiselle?' asked Poirot. 'There might be an innocent reason. You see, Mademoiselle, something *was* thrown into the water last night – something that was not innocent.'

Race held out the shawl and showed the girl its contents.

'Was that – what – she was killed with?' Rosalie asked nervously. 'And you think I killed Linnet Doyle? I don't even know her. That old woman is probably half blind anyway. It wasn't me she saw. Can I go now?'

After she had left, Poirot shook his head. 'Neither of those two women was being totally honest.'

'Well, let's continue the questioning. Mrs Otterbourne is next.'

The novelist agreed with her daughter's statement about her bedtime, but she could not say whether Rosalie had left their cabin or not. Mrs Otterbourne, excited by the crime itself, expressed her belief that the motive was about sex and jealousy. Poirot explained that neither Jacqueline de Bellefort nor Simon Doyle could be the murderer, but this did not stop the novelist's romantic imagination.

'Of course. How silly of me! It was Miss Bowers! She was probably jealous of the happy couple. They had something she could never dream of having. She's just the type: unattractive, respectable, with no experience of real emotions –'

'Thank you, Mrs Otterbourne,' said Race, as he led her quickly to the door. 'Your suggestions have been very helpful. Ah, Signor Richetti, please come in.'

The Italian was very upset by the whole business. 'What a terrible thing! A woman so young and so beautiful!'

He had gone to bed very early, had read for some time and had turned his light out before eleven. He thought he had heard a splash a few hours later, but he was not sure about the time.

Race and Poirot moved on to Mr Ferguson, who answered their questions with his usual rudeness.

'What time did you go to bed last night?' asked Race.

'At about midnight, but I don't *have to* tell you anything.'

'Did you hear a shot, or something like a cork?'

'Yes, I think I did, but there were people running around, a lot of noise on the deck above, so I'm not sure what it was.'

'Did you hear a splash?'

'I think I heard a splash, but with all the noise I can't be sure. But I'm sorry that I missed the opportunity to join in the good work. Mrs Doyle did nothing for the world.'

After Ferguson left, Poirot asked, 'You don't think he is the man *you* are looking for?'

'I don't think so. I quite like him. But one job at a time. Let's talk to Pennington.'

Andrew Pennington walked into the room, wearing a black tie.

'Gentlemen,' he said sadly, 'this business has really shocked me! Little Linnet!'

Race said, 'Mr Pennington, did you hear anything last night?'

'I heard some noise outside Dr Bessner's cabin at about midnight. He's next door at number forty. But it didn't mean anything to me at the time. After that I went to sleep and didn't hear anything else. Of course you know there'd been an affair between Simon Doyle and that girl Jacqueline de Bellefort in the past. *Cherchez la femme** – that's always a good rule.'

'But, you see, it is quite impossible that Jacqueline de Bellefort shot Madame Doyle,' said Poirot, explaining that the nurse had been with her all night. 'And so, Monsieur, we must still find the murderer, and we hope you will be able to help us. You knew more about her than her new husband did. You would, perhaps, know if she had any enemies.'

Pennington passed his tongue over rather dry-looking lips and said nervously, 'I have no idea … She was brought up in England and I know very little of her life there.'

'But there was someone on the boat who wanted to remove

* *Cherchez la femme*: French for 'Look for the woman.'

Madame Doyle. You remember that she had a fortunate escape when the rock almost hit her. But, you were not there, perhaps?' asked Poirot.

'No, I was inside the temple at the time. I heard about it afterwards, of course. Possibly an accident, don't you think?' Pennington wiped his face with an expensive handkerchief.

Race went on, 'Mr Doyle says that someone on the boat had a complaint against her family. A former friend of her father's?'

'I've no idea about that,' said Pennington, looking surprised. 'I'm very sorry that I can't help you.'

After Pennington had left, Race lit a cigarette and said, 'Mr Pennington was not at all comfortable.'

'And,' Poirot added, 'he was nervous enough to tell a rather stupid lie. He was *not* in the temple of Abu Simbel when the rock fell. I can swear to that. I had just come from there. But for now we will treat him gently.'

'We understand each other very well, my friend,' said Race. 'I think the next problem to solve is Mrs Doyle's pearls.'

'You have a plan?'

'Yes. At the end of lunch, I will make an announcement – that the pearls have been stolen. I will ask everyone to stay in the dining-room while we search the boat. We do not want to give the thief an opportunity to get rid of the pearls.'

'Good. We now know a lot about our murder suspects, but I ask myself one question: "*Why* was the pistol thrown into the water?"'

'That's your only question?' asked Race.

'At the moment, yes. That *must* be our starting point. Tell me about the pistol. You know more about guns than I do. Would Miss Van Schuyler's velvet shawl silence the sound of a shot?'

'No, it wouldn't,' said Race. 'Even without the shawl, that pistol would make very little noise.'

'That is what I expected. And this stained handkerchief –

definitely a man's and very inexpensive. Perhaps for a man like Fleetwood?'

'Or Ferguson?' suggested Race.

'Ah, yes, but quite a *jeune fille** colour, is it not?' said Poirot. 'But it is odd ... *Cette pauvre†* Madame Doyle. Lying there so peacefully ... with the little hole in her head. You remember how she looked?'

Race looked at him curiously. 'I think you're trying to tell me something – but I have no idea what it is.'

Chapter 5 The Truth is Discovered

Poirot soon received a call to Simon Doyle's bedside.

'Monsieur Poirot, would you mind asking Jackie to come here to see me? She's only a child – and I treated her badly, and –'

Poirot found the girl in the public lounge. She looked surprised by Simon's request, and followed Poirot like a puzzled child.

In Dr Bessner's cabin, she stared at Simon, unable to speak.

'Jackie!' Simon began. 'I wanted to say – '

'Simon,' Jacqueline interrupted, 'you know I didn't kill Linnet. I – I was mad last night. Can you forgive me? Your leg, you might never walk again ... '

'Jackie, stop worrying and don't exaggerate. The doctors will take care of me when we get to Assuan. I'll be as good as new.'

Jacqueline rushed forward and knelt by Simon's bed, burying her face and crying softly. Simon seemed embarrassed.

As he left Bessner's cabin, Poirot heard Jackie whisper, 'How could I be such a devil? Oh, Simon! I'm so awfully sorry.'

Then, outside on the deck, he heard a line of another

* *jeune fille*: French for 'young girl'
† *cette pauvre:* French for 'this poor girl'

conversation. 'Ungrateful daughter! After all I've done for you!'

Poirot knocked at the door of the Otterbournes' cabin. Rosalie appeared, looking very pale, with dark circles under her eyes.

'May I have the pleasure of a few minutes' conversation, Mademoiselle?'

They walked along the deck.

'Well?' she asked crossly.

'Mademoiselle, as a friend I am very worried about you. The weight of your secrets will harm you.'

'I don't know what you're talking about.'

'Mademoiselle, I know that your mother drinks and I am guessing that she found a way to hide her bottles of alcohol from you, but you discovered them last night. You waited until she was asleep and then threw the bottles into the Nile. I am right, am I not?'

'Yes!' Rosalie whispered sadly. 'I've tried so hard to protect her. Her books don't sell any more. People are tired of all that cheap sex stuff … It hurt her terribly. And so she began to drink. Then she began to dislike me because I tried to stop her.'

'*Pauvre petite*,'* said Poirot.

'Don't feel sorry for me. It's easier if you're not. But I'm so tired, and you're so kind, and I'm afraid I've been so rude to you.'

'*La politesse*,† it is not necessary between friends. But I have two more questions. At what time did you throw the bottles into the river, and did you see Mademoiselle Van Schuyler?'

'I think it was after one o'clock, but I saw nobody.'

Monsieur Poirot thought about Rosalie's answers as he walked slowly towards the dining-room for lunch.

Tim Allerton was already at the table with his mother. 'Why

* *pauvre petite*: French for 'poor little one'
† *la politesse*: French for 'politeness'

did we come on this awful trip?' he complained.

'I don't know,' agreed Mrs Allerton sadly. 'That beautiful girl! Such a *waste*. And the other one. So terribly unhappy.'

'Jacqueline? Perhaps she will learn not to fire pistols at people. Now we're all involved in a murder case!' complained Tim. 'The police will be waiting to question us at Shellal or Assuan. We're all suspects. And Ferguson told me that Linnet's pearls are missing.'

'Her pearls? I suppose that was the motive for the murder.'

'Why? Mother, you're mixing up two quite different things.'

Poirot joined the Allertons, apologizing for being late. He sat down and ordered a bottle of wine.

'We have fixed habits,' Mrs Allerton noted. 'You always drink wine. Tim drinks beer, and I drink water. But we were talking about Linnet's pearls: Ferguson told Tim that they have been stolen. Tim worries that it will[1] mean more unpleasantness for all of us.'

Poirot turned to Tim and said, 'Ah! You have had previous experience, perhaps? You have been in a house where there has been a robbery?'

'Never,' said Tim.

'Oh, yes, darling, you were at the Portarlingtons' when that awful woman's diamonds were stolen,' reminded his mother.

'Mother, you always get things wrong. I was there when they discovered that the diamonds she was wearing were false. The real ones had probably been stolen months before. Some people even thought she had sold them herself.'

'Did Joanna suggest that? She knew them quite well.'

'She wasn't there that weekend, Mother,' Tim said quietly.

Poirot politely changed the subject and talked about sending some gifts back to England. 'Can I depend on the post between here and England? Have you had any experience of it?'

'Tim gets books sometimes and has no trouble with them.'

'Ah, no, books are different,' commented Poirot.

After coffee had been served, Colonel Race stood up, explained that Mrs Doyle's pearls were missing and asked everyone to stay in the dining-room while the boat was searched.

Race and Poirot waited on the deck. They expected someone to come out, but were surprised a few minutes later when Miss Bowers came to the door of the dining-room and asked to speak to them. They went to the office.

Very calmly the nurse said, 'I want to return these.'

She took out a string of pearls and laid them on the table.

'This is most extraordinary,' Race said, as he picked up the pearls. 'Will you kindly explain, Miss Bowers?'

'Of course. I hesitated because I had to think of the family, but I could not be found with the pearls in my possession.'

'Did you take the pearls from Mrs Doyle's cabin?'

'Me? Oh, no. Miss Van Schuyler did. She can't help it, and she never admits that she's taken anything. She usually takes jewellery – and pearls are her favourite. It's my job to watch her. She always hides the things she takes in her underwear drawer, so I check the drawer every morning and return things to their owners. I found these this morning, but when I tried to return them to Mrs Doyle's cabin, there was a guard and it was impossible.' She looked worried.

'Thank you for coming to us so quickly,' said Poirot, 'but please, one more question. Miss Van Schuyler has problems, you say? Is it possible for her to commit murder?'

Miss Bowers' answer came immediately: 'Oh, no! Nothing of that kind. The old lady wouldn't hurt a fly.'

Poirot had a final question: 'Is Miss Van Schuyler at all deaf? Do you think, for example, that she could hear someone moving about in the cabin next to hers – in Mrs Doyle's cabin?'

'As a matter of fact, she *is* quite deaf, Monsieur Poirot. I don't think she could hear anything at all.'

When Miss Bowers had returned to the dining-room, Race said, 'Miss Van Schuyler must be a suspect now. Did she murder Mrs Doyle to get the pearls? I doubt it, but ...'

'I think she *did* see Rosalie Otterbourne, but I don't think she *heard* anything in Linnet Doyle's cabin. I think she was just watching for her chance to go in and take the pearls.'

'But if Mrs Doyle was shot at about ten minutes past one, when the boat was very quiet, I am amazed that no one heard the shot. Of course her husband's cabin was empty and Miss Van Schuyler is deaf. That leaves only the cabin next to her on the other side of the boat. In other words – Pennington.'

'I am promising myself the pleasure of asking him a few more questions,' said Poirot. 'But first, the pearls.'

Poirot examined the pearls carefully. He held them up to the light; he even bit one of them. Then he threw them on the table.

'Another complication, my friend,' he said. 'These pearls are not real. They are only a clever copy.'

'Are you positive?' asked Race, picking them up.

'Yes, I am certain. I was admiring Madame Doyle's pearls the first evening on the boat – they were beautiful and very real.'

'Could Miss Bowers and Miss Van Schuyler be clever jewel thieves pretending to be part of a rich American family?'

'It is difficult to say, but it would take careful planning and skill to copy Madame Doyle's pearls. It could not be done in a hurry. The person who made the copy had a good opportunity of studying the original.'

'So now we've got to find the real pearls.'

Poirot and Race searched the cabins carefully, even their own. Most cabins contained what they had expected, but there were a few surprises. Mr Ferguson's outer clothing was torn and dirty, but his underwear and handkerchiefs were of very good quality. Tim Allerton's cabin contained several pieces of religious art, including a big wooden rosary.

The two men searched both Simon's and Linnet's cabins very carefully – for clues to the theft, but also to the murder. In Linnet's room, Poirot noticed two little bottles of fingernail polish – one, labelled 'Rose', had only a drop or two of dark red liquid at the bottom; the other, labelled 'Cardinal', was nearly full. Poirot opened both bottles and the smell of pear drops filled the room.

'There is something a little curious here,' said Poirot. 'I must ask the maid.'

'I wonder where she is,' said Race.

In Dr Bessner's cabin, they found Simon Doyle looking feverish and much worse than earlier. He was surprised that they wanted to search Bessner's cabin, but Poirot explained, 'Anyone could come into this room and hide something when you are asleep.'

The next cabin was Pennington's, where they found a case full of legal and business documents.

'These seem to be all right,' commented Poirot.

'Yes,' agreed Race, 'but perhaps he destroyed any papers that connected him to murder or theft.'

Poirot lifted a heavy pistol from a drawer, looked at it and put it back. 'It seems that many people still travel with guns.'

'But Linnet Doyle wasn't shot with something that size.' Race paused and then added, 'I have an idea about the murder weapon. Perhaps the murderer left it in Linnet's cabin, and then someone else took it away and threw it into the river.'

'Yes, but who was that second person? The only other person who we know went into the cabin was Mademoiselle Van Schuyler. Would she remove the pistol? For what reason? To protect Jacqueline de Bellefort? It does not seem likely.'

'Perhaps she was worried when she saw her shawl, and threw it and its contents into the river,' suggested Race.

'It is not a satisfactory solution,' said Poirot as they left Linnet's cabin. 'I must have a few more words with Simon Doyle.'

'Monsieur Poirot, I'm glad you have returned,' Simon said. 'I'm perfectly sure that Linnet's pearls were all right yesterday. She loved them. She would recognise a copy.'

'That is probably true, but the copy was very good. Tell me, did Madame Doyle ever lend the pearls to a friend?'

'I hadn't known Linnet very long, but she was generous with her things. Perhaps she let friends wear them sometimes.'

'She never, for example, lent them to Jacqueline de Bellefort?'

Simon turned red and tried to sit up but fell back on the bed.

'Jackie is not a thief – I swear she isn't.'

'I see my suggestion has excited your anger.'

Poirot remembered a girl's voice by the Nile in Assuan saying, 'I love Simon – and he loves me … ' Perhaps her words were closer to the truth than anything else that Poirot had heard that night.

Race came to the door and reported that the passengers in the dining-room had been searched. Nothing unusual had been found.

'The Italian gentleman complained about the search. Something about his honour. And he's also carrying a gun. A big automatic.'

'Richetti has a hot temper,' said Simon. 'He was upset and rude to Linnet at Wadi Halfa because of a mistake over a telegram.'

'And Miss Rosalie Otterbourne had a little pistol in her handbag – a very small one with a pearl handle,' Race reported.

'So many guns on this boat! And Louise Bourget?'

'She's disappeared,' said Race. 'And she's one person who had time to copy the pearls. Let's have a look at her cabin.'

Poirot and Race went to the deck below and found Louise

Bourget's cabin in quite a mess. They looked through everything carefully, and then Race's attention was attracted by a shoe that he could see half under the bed. He whistled softly.

'*Qu'est-ce qu'il y a?*'* asked Poirot.

'Miss Bourget hasn't disappeared. She's here, under the bed. A knife wound to the heart. Death was immediate, probably about an hour ago, but let's find Bessner.'

Poirot bent down and picked up the right hand. He removed the corner of a hundred-pound note and showed it to Race.

'Blackmail,' said Race. 'She knew who the murderer was.'

'We have been fools!' cried Poirot. 'She *did* hear something in the night, came up, and saw the murderer leaving Madame Doyle's cabin. She saw her chance to make a lot of money.'

'But what happened here?'

'The murderer gave her the money and watched her as she counted it. Then he struck, took the money and escaped – not noticing that one of the notes was torn.'

'We may get him that way,' suggested Race doubtfully.

'No,' said Poirot. 'I think this murderer has courage and intelligence. He will notice the note and throw it away.'

After examining the body, Dr Bessner showed Poirot and Race one of his own medical knives.

'This is the type of knife that killed Mademoiselle Bourget. It is long and thin and very sharp.'

'And none of your knives are missing, Doctor?' asked Race.

'Of course not! Do you believe that I, with my important patients and my fame, would murder a worthless maid?'

Race and Poirot left quietly and Monsieur Poirot turned to the left. He heard laughter coming from Rosalie Otterbourne's cabin and saw her and Jacqueline de Bellefort chatting together.

'You are talking about scandal, Mesdemoiselles?'

* *Qu'est-ce qu'il y a?*: French for 'What is it?'

'No, of course not,' said Rosalie. 'We were comparing lipsticks.'

But Jacqueline had noticed Poirot's serious expression and asked, 'Has something happened – what has happened now?'

'You are correct. There has been another death.'

Watching them carefully, Poirot saw alarm and fear in Rosalie's eyes. Then, as the detective had expected, the girl reacted nervously when he described the murder. He led her out to the deck.

'Why do you not tell me *all* the truth, Mademoiselle?'

'What do you mean? I told you everything this morning.'

'You did not tell me that you carry a little pistol in your handbag, and you did not tell me all that you saw last night.'

'I haven't got a pistol. Here, look in my handbag.'

Poirot opened Rosalie's bag. 'No, it is not there.'

'You were wrong, and you're wrong about the other thing.'

'No, I do not think so. I think you saw a man come out of Linnet Doyle's cabin last night. You watched him walk along the deck and enter one of the two end cabins. Am I right, Mademoiselle?'

Rosalie hesitated. Then her lips opened: 'I saw nobody.'

Jacqueline saw Miss Bowers come out of Dr Bessner's cabin and rushed over to speak to her.

'How is Simon?' she demanded. 'Is he going to die?'

'He should be in hospital,' said the nurse. 'He's had too much excitement today and his temperature has risen again.'

Poirot saw Jacqueline's face and guided her into her cabin. She sat on her bed, with tears running down her cheeks.

'He'll die! And I killed him! And I love him so!'

'Too much … ' whispered Poirot to himself, remembering his thoughts in Monsieur Blondin's restaurant many months ago.

The girl's eyes brightened. 'Simon will go to hospital and they'll give him the proper treatment and everything will be all right.'

'You speak like a child. "And they lived happily ever after?"'

'No, Monsieur, nothing like that. Simon is just sorry for me now because he knows how sorry I am that I hurt him so badly.'

'Pity is a generous reaction,' Poirot said sympathetically.

Colonel Race met Poirot on the deck.

'Poirot! I've got an idea. There's something about the Italian's telegram –'

'Yes, the telegram is important,' Poirot said thoughtfully.

'You have an idea too?'

'It is more than an idea. *I am sure.* It is clear – so clear. But there are difficulties – But first, let us examine the matter of the telegram. We must talk to Monsieur Doyle one more time.'

Dr Bessner was not happy to see Race and Poirot again, but he left and Simon asked, 'What is it?'

Race said, 'Tell us again about Signor Richetti and the telegram.'

'When we came back from the Second Cataract, Linnet saw a telegram on the board. The writing was not clear and she thought it was for "Ridgeway", so she opened it. Signor Richetti saw her and pulled it out of her hand very rudely.'

'And do you know what was in the telegram?'

'Yes, Linnet read some of it aloud. It said – '

Simon paused. There was a lot of noise outside the cabin.

'Where are Monsieur Poirot and Colonel Race?' a woman shouted. 'I must speak to them *immediately*. I have important information.'

Bessner had not closed the door. Mrs Otterbourne pushed the curtain to one side and entered the room like a tropical storm. She was shaky on her legs, her face was red and she could not completely control her words. But in a clear theatrical voice she announced, 'Mr Doyle, I know who killed your wife!' The three men stared at her. 'I *saw* the person who killed Louise Bourget, so I know who also killed Mrs Doyle.'

Simon, feverish, shouted loudly, 'Please, Mrs Otterbourne, start at the beginning. You know who killed Louise Bourget?'

Mrs Otterbourne looked proudly at her audience, enjoying the idea that she would be famous for solving the mystery.

'I was on my way to the dining-room when I remembered that I had arranged to – er – meet someone. I left my daughter and went along the lower deck.'

The curtain across the door moved again, but no one noticed. Then a grey metal object appeared between the curtain and the door.

'The girl – Louise Bourget – looked out of her cabin, but seemed disappointed to see me and closed her door again. I continued to my meeting, bought – er –what I had ordered and turned round. As I walked along the deck, I saw someone knock on Miss Bourget's door and go inside.'

Race said: 'And that person was – ?'

Bang!

Mrs Otterbourne fell to the floor with a crash. From just behind her ear, the blood poured from a neat round hole.

Poirot made a catlike jump for the door and saw a big, heavy gun on the floor. Racing towards the front of the boat, he met Tim Allerton, who was hurrying round the corner.

'What was that?' cried Tim breathlessly.

'Did you meet anyone on your way here?' asked Poirot.

'Meet anyone? No.'

They found a crowd gathered at the door of Bessner's cabin: Rosalie, Jacqueline, Cornelia, Ferguson, Fanthorp and Mrs Allerton.

'I think we've seen this gun recently,' said Race.

He knocked on the door of Pennington's cabin, but there was no answer. Race went in and checked the top drawer. The gun was gone.

He and Poirot found Pennington on the deck below. He was in a small sitting-room writing letters. He lifted his face.

'Anything new?' he asked.

'Didn't you hear a shot?'

'Well – now you mention it – I believe I heard a kind of bang. But I didn't imagine – who's been shot?'

'Mrs Otterbourne – with your gun.'

'Gentlemen, I've been here for the last twenty minutes. Anyway, how could I go to the deck above, shoot this poor woman and come down here again with no one seeing me?'

'How do you explain the fact that your gun was used?'

'Well, I'm afraid that one evening in the public lounge, I mentioned that I always carry a gun with me when I travel. But why would anyone want to shoot Mrs Otterbourne?'

'She said that she had seen someone go into Louise Bourget's cabin. Before she could name the person, she was shot dead.'

Pennington wiped his face with a very fine handkerchief.

Poirot said, 'I need to discuss a few more points with you, sir. Will you come to my cabin in half an hour's time?'

'I would be delighted.'

He stood up and left the room.

'He didn't *look* very delighted,' Race said.

Poirot went on deck and found a group of passengers discussing recent events.

'Monsieur Poirot,' began Cornelia, 'how did the person who shot Mrs Otterbourne get away without us seeing him?'

'Ah,' said Poirot. 'We know he didn't go to the left or to the right, but there was one more possibility.'

Everyone looked confused, and then Jacqueline said, 'Of course – he couldn't go *up*, but he could go *down*.'

Poirot smiled. 'You have brains, Mademoiselle. The murderer could avoid the inside passage by jumping to the deck below.'

'Amazing! I suppose he'd have to be wonderfully quick,' said Cornelia. 'Three deaths … It's like living in a bad dream.'

Ferguson heard her and spoke to her angrily: 'It's the *future* that matters, not the past. Those three women were not important – Linnet Doyle and her money! A French maid, looking after her needs! A novelist with tired old ideas! I think it's a good thing that they're dead!'

'You're wrong!' Cornelia shouted at him. 'Those three women were loved by someone. And Linnet Doyle – when anything so beautiful is dead, it's a loss to the whole world.'

'You're unbelievable,' Ferguson said. He turned to Poirot. 'Do you know, sir, that Cornelia's father was almost ruined by Melhuish Ridgeway? But does she hate his daughter when she meets her? No, she admires her beauty! She forgives everything.'

'I didn't forgive her immediately,' said Cornelia softly. 'Daddy was very unhappy when he died. But didn't you just say that we should be concerned with the future, not the past? All that was in the past, wasn't it?'

'You *have* understood me,' said Ferguson. 'Cornelia Robson, you're the nicest woman I've ever met. Will you marry me?'

'You're crazy.'

'I am perfectly serious, and Monsieur Poirot is my witness. For you, I will even accept the conditions of a marriage contract.'

'Never. You laugh at all sorts of serious things: education, art, culture – and death. I could never trust you,' Cornelia said, red-faced, rushing off to her cabin.

'I think she really means it,' said Ferguson. Then he looked at Poirot. 'What's the matter? You seem deep in thought.'

'Monsieur Ferguson, you are a very rude young man.'

'Yes. But what do you think of that girl? She's got spirit, hasn't she? Perhaps I can get to her through her old cousin.'

He left to find Miss Van Schuyler.

Poirot followed. He sat in the public lounge at a distance from Ferguson and Miss Van Schuyler, but he could hear their conversation clearly.

'Miss Van Schuyler, I want to marry your cousin.'

'This suggestion is beyond consideration, young man,' the old lady said. 'You are obviously not good enough for her. You have no social position. Now go away!'

'I've got two arms, two legs, good health and a reasonable brain. That's more important than a social position.'

Ferguson smiled and walked calmly out of the lounge.

Poirot spoke to the old woman: 'He's a bit strange – most of the family are. You recognised him, I suppose? Calls himself Ferguson and won't use his title because of his political ideas.'

'His *title*?' asked Miss Van Schuyler sharply.

'Yes, that's young Lord Dawlish. Very wealthy, graduated from Oxford University. Rather extreme ideas now, though.'

Poirot could almost see the thoughts going through Miss Van Schuyler's brain before she left the lounge.

Poirot's own thoughts became serious again.

'*Mais oui*,' he said at last. 'It all fits.'

Colonel Race found him sitting alone.

'My dear friend,' Poirot said, 'please bring young Fanthorp here.'

When Fanthorp was sitting in front of him, Poirot began his questions. 'Monsieur, I have an impression of you because I understand a little about English gentlemen. I know that there are "things which are done" and "things which are not done".'

Jim Fanthorp smiled.

'I believe that one "thing which is not done" is to listen to other people's private conversations, but the other day I observed as you listened to a conversation between the Doyles and Mr Pennington. You interrupted them and gave Madame Doyle some advice about signing legal documents – that is not what a

75

gentleman would do. Also, you work for a small law firm near Wode Hall, and I doubt that you can afford this trip. So – what is the reason for your presence on this boat? Remember that there have been three murders.'

Fanthorp seemed unable to speak.

'If I add that the weapon used to kill Madame Otterbourne was a gun owned by Andrew Pennington, will you understand that it is your duty to tell us all you can?'

Fanthorp thought for a moment, and then spoke. 'My uncle, Mrs Doyle's English lawyer, suspected that Mrs Doyle's American trustee, Mr Pennington, had been using her money for his own profit.'

'In plain language,' said Race, 'your uncle suspected that Pennington had stolen it?'

'Yes. In a letter, Mrs Doyle told us that she had met Pennington by accident while on her honeymoon. I was sent to watch them because neither Mrs Doyle nor Mr Pennington knew me. On the occasion you mentioned, I had to behave badly, but I was satisfied with the result.'

'Another question,' said Poirot. 'Who would it be easier to cheat – Madame Doyle or her husband?'

'Mr Doyle,' said Fanthorp with a smile. 'He would trust his advisers and sign anything they gave him.'

'I agree,' said Poirot. He looked at Race. 'There's a motive, and I think we may get the proof from Pennington himself. Thank you for your help, Mr Fanthorp.'

Two minutes later, Andrew Pennington appeared.

'Mr Pennington, we know that you had known Linnet since she was a small child and that you and her father were close friends. So close, in fact, that on his death you were appointed as trustee to the enormous fortune he left her?'

'Yes,' Pennington answered cautiously. 'My partner and I.'

'Linnet would take control of her fortune – worth millions

– on her twenty-first birthday or when she married.'

Pennington said angrily, 'This is none of your business, and I don't understand the relationship between this and Linnet's murder.'

Poirot leaned forward, his eyes green and catlike. 'In considering motives, financial matters are always important. I was wondering if Mademoiselle Ridgeway's marriage caused alarm in your office? Perhaps her financial affairs were not in perfect order and you hurried to Cairo to meet her "accidentally"?'

'That's crazy! I didn't even know that Linnet was married until I met her in Cairo. I was totally surprised. Her letter reached New York after I had departed on the *Carmanic*.'

'It is strange,' said Poirot, 'that the only recent labels on your luggage of a voyage across the Atlantic are from the *Normandie*, which, I remember, sailed two days after the *Carmanic*.'

'We've good reason for believing that you received Mrs Doyle's letter before you left New York,' said Race.

Pennington sat down. 'You're too clever for me, gentlemen. But I had my reasons for lying to you. I think Linnet's English lawyers were stealing money from her. I came over to check.'

'But why did you lie about the letter from Mrs Doyle?'

'Well, I didn't want to turn their honeymoon into a business trip, so I made the meeting accidental. And I didn't know anything about this Doyle – perhaps he was part of the theft.'

Poirot leaned forwards. 'Monsieur, we believe that Linnet Ridgeway's unexpected marriage put you in a difficult financial position. You hurried to Cairo to get her signature on some important documents, but you failed. Then at Abu Simbel, you pushed a large rock down towards her, but you missed your object.

'Then you had another unexpected opportunity on the return journey. If Madame Doyle were murdered, everyone would suspect Mademoiselle de Bellefort. And we *know* that your gun killed Mrs Otterbourne, who was prepared to tell us the name of the person she believed had killed both women –'

'Are you crazy? I wouldn't gain anything from Linnet's death. Her money goes to her husband. *He's* the one with a motive.'

Race said coldly, 'Doyle was shot that night. He couldn't even stand up without help. He couldn't leave the lounge and kill someone. As you say, Doyle would receive his wife's fortune, but he knows nothing about her financial affairs. He would trust her old advisors. I think you *would* gain from such circumstances. Are you ready to tell us the truth?'

Pennington's hands were shaking, but before he left the room he said, 'You don't understand. The stock market went mad, but with a little luck everything will be OK by the end of June. I am innocent, gentlemen. I did not push that rock at Abu Simbel on purpose – it was an accident – and I did not shoot Linnet.'

Alone again, Race said to Poirot, 'We got more from Pennington than I expected. We can connect him to the rock and to a motive for Mrs Doyle's murder, but there's no proof.'

'No proof yet,' said Poirot rather mysteriously. 'But there is my conversation with Mademoiselle de Bellefort in the garden at Assuan. Tim Allerton's and Louise Bourget's answers to our questions. Two bottles of nail polish. My bottle of wine. The shawl. The handkerchief with the pink stain. The deaths of Louise and Mrs Otterbourne. The gun left at the scene of the last murder. One thing is clear: Pennington didn't do it!'

'What?'

'Pennington is clever and he had the motive. He even tried to murder her. But he is not bold enough. This crime was dangerous and needed courage and speed. And imagination.'

Race looked at him with the respect one able man gives to another. 'So you've solved it?'

'I think so, but there are one or two things that I must find out. We'll need to speak to Tim Allerton again.'

Tim Allerton came quickly when he was sent for.

'At our first meeting, Mr Allerton,' Poirot said seriously, 'you mentioned Mademoiselle Joanna Southwood. After studying several cases, a friend of mine, a detective at Scotland Yard, has recently connected her with certain jewellery thefts.

'Mademoiselle Southwood visits her wealthy friends, borrows a piece of jewellery, has it copied and returns the original. After some time, when she is far away, her partner visits the same person, exchanges the copy for the real piece and leaves with the other jewellery. No one notices for some time and so the two thieves are unlikely to be connected to the crime.

'I believe you are Joanna Southwood's partner. The missing ring in Majorca. A house party when another piece of jewellery disappeared. Your dislike of your mother's friendship with me. And then the copy of Madame Doyle's pearls is returned to us. We had to wonder where the real pearls were, didn't we?'

Tim Allerton went very pale. 'You have no proof that I'm a thief.'

Poirot answered slowly, 'I have a good idea that the pearls are hidden in your rosary. I am guessing that Mademoiselle Southwood had them copied some time ago. She knew about the Doyles' honeymoon and sent the copy to you inside a book.'

There was long pause. Then Tim said quietly, 'You win! It's been a good game, but I know it's finished now.'

'Do you realise that you were seen last night when you went into Madame Doyle's cabin to steal the pearls?'

'Listen – I'm a thief, not a murderer! Who saw me?'

'Rosalie Otterbourne saw you leave Linnet Doyle's cabin just after one in the morning.'

'So it was she who told you,' Tim said rather sadly.

Poirot said gently, 'Excuse me; she did not tell me. I am Hercule Poirot. I do not need to be told. Rosalie Otterbourne lied. She said, "I saw nobody." She wanted to protect you.'

Tim said, a different note in his voice, 'She's an extraordinary girl. She's been through some difficult times with her mother. But now you know about the pearls, what are you going to do?'

Poirot asked Race to bring Rosalie Otterbourne to their meeting.

When she arrived, looking anxious, Poirot said, 'I know that Monsieur Allerton is not the murderer, and if you continue to say you saw nobody last night, there is no case against him.'

Poirot turned to Tim Allerton. 'Monsieur Allerton, the copy of Madame Doyle's pearls is in a little box on the table by the door. Perhaps you would like to examine them?'

Tim got up. He understood what Poirot was saying.

'Thanks!' he said. 'You won't have to give me another chance!'

He picked up the little box as he and Rosalie left the room. When he was outside he opened it, took out the false pearls and threw them into the Nile.

'There!' he said. 'They're gone. When I return the box to Poirot, the real string of pearls will be inside. I've been a terrible fool!'

'But why did you do it?'

'How did I start?' Tim said. 'I was bored and lazy, and I enjoyed the risk, I suppose. You'd never steal, would you?'

'No, I don't think so, but I think I understand.'

'You're so lovely ... Why didn't you say you'd seen me last night?'

'I thought they might suspect you, and I knew you weren't a murderer.' She put out a shy hand and touched his arm.

'Rosalie, would you – you know what I mean? Or will you always hate me for being a thief?'

She smiled. 'I've done things I'm ashamed of too. But this Joanna – is she special to you?'

'I don't care about Joanna! She's a most unattractive woman.'

Back in the public lounge, Race was becoming impatient with

his friend. '*Do* you know who committed the three murders on this boat or *don't* you? We know it wasn't Pennington or young Allerton or, I suppose, Fleetwood. Please tell me who it was.'

But at that moment Cornelia and Dr Bessner came in. The girl had just heard about her cousin's habit of stealing things, and wanted to be sure that it would remain a secret.

'It would destroy the family if people knew,' she said. 'Dr Bessner says that there's a wonderful treatment for this condition.'

'Don't worry,' said Race with a humourless smile. 'We're very good at keeping secrets.'

'Dr Bessner,' said Poirot, 'how is your patient?'

'He is doing well. But, still, this Miss de Bellefort worries about him all day. Why? One minute she shoots him, the next she is worried whether he will live or die.' He turned to Cornelia. 'If *you* loved a man, you would not shoot him. No, you are sensible.'

Race interrupted this interesting and affectionate scene. 'Since Doyle is all right, can I interview him again? He was telling us about a telegram.'

'Ho, ho, ho, that was very funny! Doyle told me it was a telegram all about vegetables – potatoes, beans, onions … '

'My God,' Race said. 'It's Richetti! Those words were used in the South African war. Potatoes mean machine guns, beans mean bombs … Richetti is a very dangerous man. He's killed more than once and he'll kill again. Is he our man?'

'Richetti is *your* man,' Poirot said, 'but he did not kill Linnet Doyle. I have half of the proof I need to point to her murderer, but I must wait for the other half.'

'But aren't you going to tell us?' cried Cornelia.

'*Mais oui,*' he said, 'I like an audience. I like to say, "See how clever Hercule Poirot is!"'

'Well,' said Race gently, 'how clever *is* Hercule Poirot?'

'At first I was very stupid. I could not understand why Jacqueline de Bellefort's pistol had been taken away from the scene of the crime. Finally, I understood. The murderer took it away because he *had* to take it away – because he had not finished with it.'

Poirot leaned towards Race. 'You and I, my friend, decided that Linnet Doyle's murderer had seen a chance and had acted without much planning, knowing that everyone would blame Jacqueline de Bellefort for the murder after what had happened between her and Simon Doyle.

'But if that idea is wrong, the whole case changes. Every detail of the crime – even putting a strong sleeping drug in my wine – was very carefully planned and accurately timed long before the *Karnak* began its journey up the Nile.

'My first clue was when the pistol, wrapped in Miss Van Schuyler's shawl, was pulled from the Nile. If the murderer wanted to point the finger at Mademoiselle de Bellefort, he had to leave the pistol in Madame Doyle's cabin.'

Poirot turned towards Dr Bessner. 'You, Dr Bessner, told us that the skin around the bullet hole on Linnet Doyle's head was burned and black. But this would not have happened if the pistol had been wrapped in a shawl.

'But a bullet from the pistol *had* been fired through the shawl. Jacqueline certainly did not use the shawl when she fired the pistol at Simon. It appeared, therefore, that a *third* shot had been fired – one we knew nothing about. That was difficult to explain.

'Then in Linnet Doyle's cabin I found two nail polish bottles, but when I smelled the contents, I found that one contained nail polish and the other contained red ink. It suggested a connection with the handkerchief with the pink stain, which had been wrapped round the pistol. Red ink washes out quickly but always leaves a pale pink stain.

'And the picture became even clearer when Louise Bourget

was murdered. This morning I asked her if she had seen anything the previous night. Her answer was unusually long and complicated. What did that tell us?'

'That she *had* climbed the stairs,' suggested Race.

'No, it told me that she was sending a message to someone in the room. I knew that the message was not for me or you, Race, so it had to be for Dr Bessner or for Simon Doyle. Mademoiselle Bourget could easily speak to you, Dr Bessner, in private, but this was the only time she could speak to Monsieur Doyle. She wanted him to understand her message and to tell her not to worry – and he did.'

'But Mr Doyle wasn't in Mrs Doyle's cabin. It was *impossible* for him to leave the lounge with the wound to his leg,' said Dr Bessner.

'Impossible, I know, but he did. It was the only logical meaning to Louise Bourget's words. Then I remembered that there had been five minutes when Simon was alone in the lounge before Dr Bessner arrived. During that time, what do we know about Simon Doyle's injury?

'Two people see Mademoiselle de Bellefort fire her pistol. They also see Simon Doyle fall across a chair and put a handkerchief against his leg. The handkerchief turns red. Then Mr Doyle insists that Mademoiselle Robson takes Mademoiselle de Bellefort to her cabin, and he asks Fanthorp to find Dr Bessner. When he is alone, Simon acts quickly. He picks up the pistol from under the sofa, takes off his shoes, runs to his wife's cabin, shoots her in the head, leaves the bottle with red ink beside her bottle of nail polish, runs back to the lounge, picks up Mademoiselle Van Schuyler's shawl, which he has hidden in his chair, wraps it around the pistol and shoots himself in the leg. He falls into the chair near a window and throws the pistol – wrapped in the handkerchief and the shawl – into the Nile.'

'Impossible!' said Race.

'Not *impossible*. Remember that Tim Allerton heard a pop – *followed* by a splash. And he heard the sound of a man running past his door. It was Simon Doyle running past his cabin.'

Race objected, 'It's impossible. Doyle couldn't think that quickly. He hasn't got the brains for it.'

'But he has the body for quick actions – someone else did the thinking for him. It was a very cleverly planned piece of work. It could not be by *chance* that Simon Doyle had a bottle of red ink in his pocket. It was not *chance* that Jacqueline de Bellefort's foot kicked the pistol under the sofa, where it would be forgotten until later.'

'Jacqueline?'

'Certainly. The two halves of the murder. The shot fired by Jacqueline gave Simon his alibi. Simon's insistence that she should not be left alone gave Jacqueline *hers*. Her brains – his speed and timing.

'If you realise that they are still lovers, it is all clear. Simon goes away with his rich wife, kills her, gets her money and after a certain amount of time, marries his true love.

'Everything was part of their plan. Jacqueline following the new couple. Simon's pretended anger. And he was too affectionate towards his wife in public – not like an ordinary Englishman. And when Jacqueline told me that someone was in the shadows, listening to our conversation, there *was* no one! Then one night on this boat, I heard Simon's voice outside my cabin. He was saying, "We've got to go on with it now." It was Doyle, but he was speaking to Jacqueline, not to Linnet.

'The final scene was perfectly planned and timed. There was a sleeping drug in my wine. There were honest witnesses to see Jacqueline shoot Simon. Then, when the doctor arrived, he really had been shot.

'But then the plan goes wrong. Louise Bourget has been unable to sleep. She comes up the stairs and sees Simon Doyle enter his wife's cabin and come out again. She understands what has happened when she sees the dead Madame Doyle the next morning. She asks for money. She knows everything, so she cannot live.'

'But it would be impossible for Simon Doyle to kill *her*,' Cornelia objected.

'Yes, but Simon asked to see Jacqueline and wanted to speak to her alone. He told her about this new danger, so Jacqueline killed Louise Bourget with one of Dr Bessner's knives before lunch and returned the knife before Dr Bessner noticed.

'Then, when Madame Otterbourne tried to tell us that she had seen Jacqueline on the lower deck, Simon shouted at her – he was warning Jacqueline. She remembered Pennington's talk about a pistol, ran to his room, found the gun and shot Madame Otterbourne. She was very quick and her cabin was only two doors from Dr Bessner's, so she did not go to the left or the right, or up or down. She simply dropped the gun and ran into her own cabin, appearing when everyone rushed out to see what had happened.'

There was a silence and then Race asked, 'What happened to the first bullet fired at Doyle by the girl?'

'I think it went into the table and Doyle removed it when he was alone and threw it out of the window. He had, of course, an extra bullet, so that it would appear that only two shots had been fired.'

Cornelia said, 'They thought of everything. It's – horrible!'

Poirot was silent. His eyes seemed to be saying, 'You are wrong. They did not take into consideration Hercule Poirot.'

◆

Much later that evening, Hercule Poirot knocked on the door of Jacqueline de Bellefort's cabin. He asked the guard to wait outside.

'Well,' Jacqueline said, 'you were too clever for us. You took Simon by surprise, and he told you everything.' She paused. 'I'm not a safe person now – killing people is so terribly easy. You begin to feel that it's only *you* that matters. You told me not to open my heart to evil. That was the moment to stop. It was still possible – Simon and I loved each other.'

'And for you love was enough, but not for him.'

'Yes, Simon wanted money so desperately – for horses, boats, sport. He's like a child – he wants things so much. But he didn't try to get money by marrying a rich wife. We met and we wanted a future together. He tried to be a successful businessman, but he failed. Then I thought I could get him a job at my dear friend's new house, but Linnet ignored our friendship and tried to steal Simon from me. That's why I'm not sorry about her, even now. Simon didn't even like her! He thought she was good-looking, but terribly bossy. One day he said, "If I had any luck, I'd marry her and she'd die in about a year and leave me the money." Then I found him reading about poisons. He had decided to kill her, but I knew he couldn't make it work, so I had to help him. We planned the details, giving each other an alibi, and it worked.'

'Yes,' said Poirot, 'but Louise Bourget couldn't sleep that night.'

'I can't believe that I did that, but Simon and I were safe except for that blackmailing girl. I gave her all the money we could find, and while she counted it, I did it! It was horribly, horribly easy . . . But even then we weren't safe. Mrs Otterbourne had seen me. But that time I had to act extremely quickly. It was almost exciting.' She stopped talking for a moment. 'Don't worry about me, Monsieur Poirot. If we had won, I'd have been very happy and enjoyed things without regrets.'

Poirot got up. Jacqueline rose too. She said with a sudden smile, 'Do you remember when I said I must follow my star? You warned me that it might be a false star.'

He went out to the deck with her laughter ringing in his ears.

♦

It was early dawn when they came into Shellal.

Poirot whispered to himself, '*Quel pays sauvage!*'[*]

Race stood beside him. 'Richetti will be taken to shore first. Then the medical people will come for Doyle. He deserves to be hanged, but I feel a bit sorry for the girl.'

Poirot shook his head. 'People say love excuses everything, but it is dangerous to love as she loved Simon Doyle. It is what I said when I saw her first. "She cares too much, that little one!"'

As Cornelia Robson joined them on the deck, Miss Van Schuyler moved slowly towards them, shouting, 'Cornelia, why aren't you helping me? I want to go directly home.'

Cornelia took a deep breath. 'I'm not going home, Cousin. I'm going to get married.'

'So you're being sensible at last,' said the old lady.

'Yes, but I'm not going to marry Ferguson – I'm going to marry Dr Bessner. He's kind and knows a lot. I've always been interested in sick people and their problems, and I shall have a wonderful life with him.'

The boat landed, and after Richetti had been marched off, Simon Doyle was carried along the deck. Jacqueline de Bellefort followed behind with a guard at her side.

'Hello, Simon!' she said.

Simon's face brightened for a moment. 'I lost my head and admitted everything, Jackie. Sorry.'

'It's all right, Simon. A fool's game and we lost. That's all.'

She bent down to tie her shoe, and when she stood up again she had something in her hand. There was a sharp 'pop'.

---

[*] *Quel pays sauvage!*: French for 'What wild country!'

Simon Doyle shook once and then lay still.

Jacqueline stood for a minute, pistol in hand, and gave Poirot a quick smile. Then she turned the little gun against her heart and fired. She fell to the floor beside Simon Doyle.

'Where did she get that pistol?' shouted Race.

Poirot felt a hand on his arm. 'You knew?' Mrs Allerton said.

'I realised that she had a pair of pistols when one was found in Rosalie Otterbourne's handbag. Jacqueline put it there when we announced our search. Later, she went to Rosalie's cabin for a chat and got it back.'

Mrs Allerton said, 'You wanted her to take that way out?'

'Yes,' admitted Poirot. 'But she would not take it alone. And so Simon Doyle has died an easier death than he deserved.'

'Love can be a very frightening thing.'

'That is why most great love stories are tragedies,' said Poirot.

Mrs Allerton looked at her son and Rosalie Otterbourne, who were standing together in the sunlight.

'But thank God, there is happiness in the world.'

When the *Karnak* reached shore, the whole world heard about the death of the famous, beautiful and wealthy Linnet Doyle. Sir George Wode read about it in his London club, Sterndale Rockford in his New York office, and Joanna Southwood in Switzerland. And in the pub in Malton-under-Wode, Mr Burnaby said, rather accurately, 'Well, it doesn't seem to have done her much good, poor girl.'

But soon they stopped talking about her and discussed horse-racing. Because, as Mr Ferguson was saying at that minute in Egypt, it is not the past that matters but the future.

ACTIVITIES

Chapter 1

Before you read

1   What do you know about Egypt? Work with a partner.

    a   Discuss the country's climate, geography and history.

    b   Based on what you know, why would Egypt be a good background for a murder mystery set in the 1930s with characters from Europe and the United States?

2   Can you name any famous detectives from literature, films or TV? What do they look like? What makes them unforgettable?

3   Look at the Word List at the back of this book. Decide if each of these sentences are true or false.

    a   Photographs of *celebrities* often appear in newspapers and popular magazines.

    b   Twenty-first-century businesses send a large number of *telegrams* every day.

    c   An *engaged* couple have been married for more than a year.

    d   A *honeymoon* follows a wedding ceremony.

    e   A *scandal* is something most people are proud of.

    f   When they are trying to solve a murder case, the police ask suspects about their *alibis*.

    g   Both men and women might wear a *velvet* jacket for a formal occasion.

    h   Most capital cities have some ancient *pyramids* near the centre.

    i   In most countries it is illegal for passengers to carry a *pistol* on an international flight.

    j   Well-organised people plan their *coincidences* very carefully.

While you read

4   Circle the correct answers.

    a   Mr Burnaby and his customer are *bored by / interested in* Linnet Ridgeway, the new owner of Wode Hall.

b Charles Windlesham loves Linnet Ridgeway *more / less* than she loves him.

c Joanna Southwood *would not / would* be a faithful friend through both good and bad times.

d Linnet Ridgeway's enquiries have *increased / ruined* her maid's chances of a happy future.

e Hercule Poirot has the impression that Jacqueline de Bellefort's celebration at Chez Ma Tante is likely to be followed by *an exciting future / disappointment*.

f Linnet Ridgeway *doesn't hesitate / hesitates* before hiring Simon Doyle as her land agent after she meets him.

g Mrs Allerton has a *high / low* opinion of Joanna Southwood.

h *Something / Nothing* worries Cornelia Robson's mother about Miss Van Schuyler's trip to Europe and Egypt.

i Linnet's American trustees and her British lawyers are *concerned / delighted* about her marriage to Simon Doyle.

j Mrs Otterbourne and her daughter Rosalie have a very *different / similar* approach to life.

After you read

5 How are these people described in this chapter?

   a Linnet Ridgeway

   b Joanna Southwood

   c Jacqueline de Bellefort

   d Simon Doyle

   e Hercule Poirot

   f Tim Allerton

   g Cornelia Robson

6 Discuss why these people might not have a high opinion of Linnet Ridgeway's decision to marry Simon Doyle.

   a Charles Windlesham

   b Jacqueline de Bellefort

   c Mrs Allerton

   d Andrew Pennington and Sterndale Rockford

Chapter 2

Before you read

7   Imagine that you are on holiday in Egypt. Which of the characters from Chapter 1 would you like to meet and chat with at your hotel? Discuss your reasons.

While you read

8   Write the names of the people who might have these thoughts after their first meeting with Hercule Poirot in Egypt.

    a   'Monsieur Poirot is quite old, but he has a sense of humour and understands human nature.'   ....

    b   'The great detective and I have many things in common. We are both famous.'   ....

    c   'How dare that little Belgian refuse to work for me! And he thinks that he understands how I really feel!'   ....

    d   'I suppose Monsieur Poirot's advice about my future is sensible, but I must make my own decisions.'   ....

    e   'Poirot's right – Jackie's got brains. But my plan will work and then I can forget about her.'   ....

9   Who is it? Match these people with the descriptions below.

    Andrew Pennington   Cornelia Robson   Rosalie Otterbourne
    Jim Fanthorp   Miss Bowers   Mrs Allerton   Mr Ferguson
    Linnet Doyle   Tim Allerton   Jacqueline de Bellefort
    Signor Richetti   Miss Van Schuyler

    a   wears the wrong clothes for the climate; hates rich people and museums   ....

    b   speaks more than one language; is offended by people who do not value ancient history and art   ....

91

c enjoys chatting with Hercule Poirot about the nature of criminal motives ....

d is old, ugly, arrogant and bossy ....

e follows orders like a slave ....

f envies other people their mothers ....

g surprises people by arriving on the *Karnak* ....

h is troubled by fears, worries and enemies, real or imagined ....

i isn't polite to a guest at his supper table ....

j has a number of important documents with him that need signatures ....

k openly admires Mrs Doyle's habit of reading documents carefully before signing them ....

l works as a secretary and nurse ....

After you read

10 Which people, places and/or situations do these characters worry about or dislike?

    a Tim Allerton

    b Rosalie Otterbourne

    c Mrs Otterbourne

    d Signor Guido Richetti

    e Mrs Allerton

    f Mr Ferguson

    g Miss Van Schuyler

    h Mr Fanthorp

    i Mr Pennington

11 Discuss why it is important for several characters to be unhappy or to have problems in a murder mystery.

Chapter 3

Before you read

12 In Chapter 2, Hercule Poirot learns about the background to the Doyles' marriage from Linnet Doyle, Jacqueline de Bellefort and Simon Doyle, and wonders whose story is nearest the truth. Which story do you believe? Which of these three characters do you feel most sympathetic towards?

While you read

13 On which of the four days covered in Chapter 3 does each of these events happen? Write 1st, 2nd, 3rd or 4th.

a A telegram arrives for Signor Richetti.   .....

b Colonel Race and Hercule Poirot learn that Simon Doyle was shot in the leg the previous night.   .....

c Most of the passengers from the *Karnak* make their first visit to the ancient temple at Abu Simbel.   .....

d Miss Van Schuyler cannot find her velvet shawl.   .....

e Colonel Race arrives on the *Karnak*.   .....

f Linnet Doyle is murdered in the early morning.   .....

g Cornelia Robson and Jim Fanthorp are witnesses when Jacqueline de Bellefort shoots Simon Doyle.   .....

h An enormous rock almost kills Linnet Doyle while she is sitting on the beach with her husband.   .....

After you read

14 Work with a partner. Are these sentences true or false according to what happens in Chapter 3? Discuss your answers and explain them with information from the story.

a Andrew Pennington seems slightly upset by at least one of Hercule Poirot's questions as they walk to Abu Simbel.

b Simon persuades Linnet to leave the temple at Abu Simbel after a short time.

c Jacqueline de Bellefort pushes the rock that almost kills Linnet.

d Immediately after the rock falls to the beach, Hercule Poirot cannot see Andrew Pennington.

e Tim Allerton and Rosalie Otterbourne admire each others' mothers.

f Signor Richetti thinks Linnet Doyle's actions are always charming.

g Colonel Race is on the *Karnak* on official business.

h Hercule Poirot tells Colonel Race that he is enjoying a pleasant, peaceful journey on the *Karnak*.

i Both Mr Ferguson and Miss de Bellefort make Cornelia Robson feel more interesting than usual.

j On the night before the murder, Hercule Poirot finds it hard to go to sleep.

k Jacqueline de Bellefort seems very upset after she fires her pistol at Simon Doyle.

l Linnet Doyle is awake when the murderer shoots her.

Chapter 4

Before you read

15 Look back at the sentences in Question 14. Which information do you think will help Hercule Poirot to solve the murder?

While you read

16 Who wanted to kill Linnet Doyle? Write the names which may be connected to the possible motives.

a Linnet stole Simon Doyle from her. ....

b Linnet refused to marry him. ....

c Linnet bought his house and made a lot of changes to it. ....

d She wanted the money she could get from Linnet's expensive pearls. ....

e His marriage to Marie was stopped by Linnet's enquiries. ....

f He wanted to cover up his use of Linnet's money for his own investments. ....

g Linnet had a romantic life that this girl could never have because she is plain. ....

h He thought the world would be
better without women like Linnet
Doyle.   ....

After you read

17 Notice where these are mentioned or referred to in this chapter.
Explain why you think Hercule Poirot and Colonel Race want to
find out more about each of them.

    a the letter 'J'

    b Jacqueline de Bellefort's pistol

    c a splash

    d a conversation between Poirot and Jacqueline de Bellefort,
       heard by someone at the Cataract Hotel

    e the passenger list

    f Linnet Doyle's pearls

    g sleeping drugs

    h a handkerchief

    i a velvet shawl

Chapter 5

Before you read

18 Divide the characters in Chapters 1–4 into three groups. Discuss
your reasons.

    a Possible murder suspects

    b People with a strong alibi

    c People who do not fit into either of group **a** or **b**

While you read

19 Four more people die violent deaths in this chapter. Complete
the information about the second and third murders as you
learn about them.

    a Second person murdered   ....

       Weapon used   ....

       Owner of the weapon   ....

       Reason for murder   ....

       ....

       Murderer   ....

b Third person murdered ....

Weapon used ....

Owner of the weapon ....

Reason for murder ....

....

Murderer ....

20 Write something that the first person likes about the second person.

a Mr Ferguson/Cornelia Robson ....

....

b Miss Van Schuyler/Mr Ferguson ....

....

c Tim Allerton/Rosalie Otterbourne ....

....

d Dr Bessner/Cornelia Robson ....

....

e Cornelia Robson/Dr Bessner ....

....

After you read

21 Work with a partner. Discuss the connection between these pairs.

a Mrs Otterbourne/the splash

b Tim Allerton/jewel thefts

c Miss Van Schuyler/Linnet Doyle's pearls

d Louise Bourget/a piece of a £100 note

e Cornelia's father/Linnet's father

f Andrew Pennington/the *Normandie*

g Signor Richetti/vegetables

h Simon Doyle/red ink

i Simon/Miss Van Schuyler's shawl

j Simon/the third bullet

k Jacqueline de Bellefort/a false star